Eyewitness
AZTEC

Peruvian mummy cloth

Aztec sacrificial knife

Mesoamerican farming tools

Ceremonial urn showing Chac, the Mayan god of rain

Aztec ceramic flute

Marigolds, given as offerings to goddesses by the Aztecs

Moche vessel showing fisherman in boat

Peruvian silver portrait beaker

Olmec jade mask

Eyewitness
AZTEC

Mortar and pestle
with chillies

Written by
ELIZABETH BAQUEDANO

Photographed by
MICHEL ZABÉ

Aztec army commander

Aztec
skull mask

Inca necklace made with
turquoise, shell, and gold beads

Toltec coyote
warrior inlaid with
mother-of-pearl

DK

Warrior wearing feather headdress

Zapotec jade
necklace

Chancay
textile doll

LONDON, NEW YORK,
MELBOURNE, MUNICH and DELHI

Project editor Christine Webb
Art editor Andrew Nash
Managing editor Helen Parker
Managing art editor Julia Harris
Production Louise Barratt
Picture research Cynthia Hole
Researcher Céline Carez
Additional photography Andy Crawford, Dave Rudkin

THIS EDITION
Editors Rob Houston, Steve Setford, Jessamy Wood
Art editors Carol Davis, Peter Radcliffe
Managing editors Julie Ferris, Jane Yorke
Managing art editor Owen Peyton Jones
Associate publisher Andrew Macintyre
Production editor Marc Staples
Jacket designer Neal Cobourne

This Eyewitness ® Guide has been conceived by
Dorling Kindersley Limited and Editions Gallimard

First published in Great Britain in 1993.
This revised edition published in Great Britain in 2011
by Dorling Kindersley Limited,
80 Strand, London WC2R 0RL

Copyright © 1993, 2006, 2011
Dorling Kindersley Limited, London
A Penguin Company

14 15 16 5 4 3

019 – 175427 – Jul/2011

A CIP catalogue record for this book is
available from the British Library.

ISBN 978-1-40534-543-9

Colour reproduction by Colourscan,
Singapore; MDP, UK

Printed and bound in China by South China
Printing Co. Ltd

Discover more at
www.dk.com

Toltec
warrior

Peruvian
feather fan

Mixtec head

Ancient Peruvian feather headdress

Contents

Chacmool from the
Great Temple of
the Aztecs

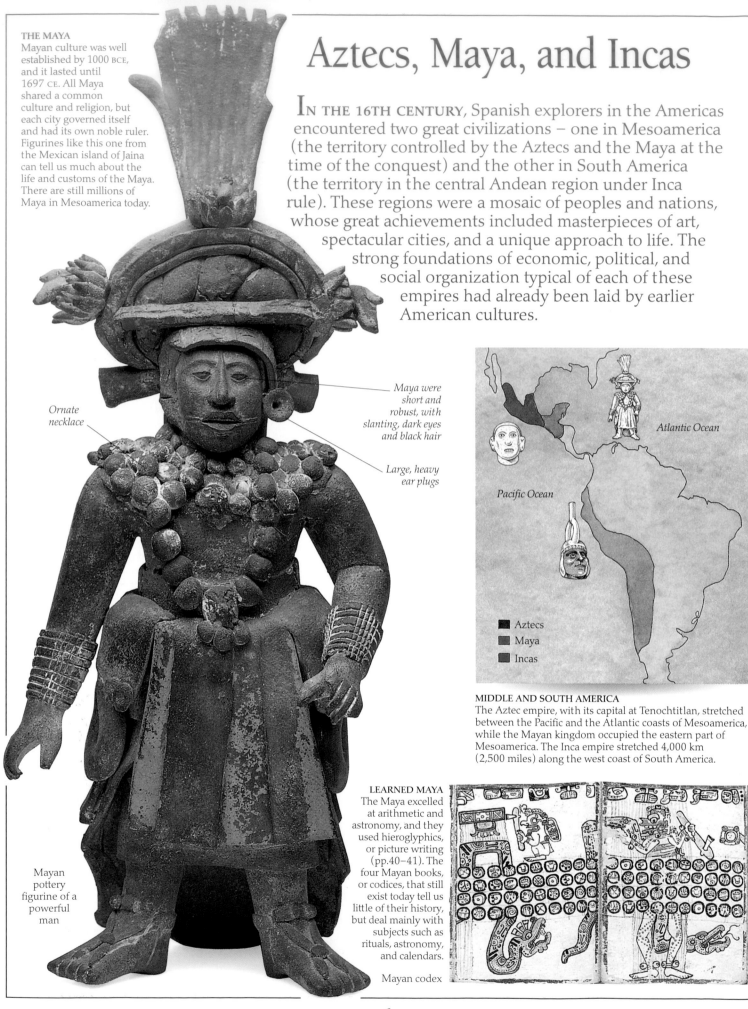

THE MAYA
Mayan culture was well established by 1000 BCE, and it lasted until 1697 CE. All Maya shared a common culture and religion, but each city governed itself and had its own noble ruler. Figurines like this one from the Mexican island of Jaina can tell us much about the life and customs of the Maya. There are still millions of Maya in Mesoamerica today.

IN THE 16TH CENTURY, Spanish explorers in the Americas encountered two great civilizations – one in Mesoamerica (the territory controlled by the Aztecs and the Maya at the time of the conquest) and the other in South America (the territory in the central Andean region under Inca rule). These regions were a mosaic of peoples and nations, whose great achievements included masterpieces of art, spectacular cities, and a unique approach to life. The strong foundations of economic, political, and social organization typical of each of these empires had already been laid by earlier American cultures.

Ornate necklace

Maya were short and robust, with slanting, dark eyes and black hair

Large, heavy ear plugs

Atlantic Ocean

Pacific Ocean

■ Aztecs
■ Maya
■ Incas

MIDDLE AND SOUTH AMERICA
The Aztec empire, with its capital at Tenochtitlan, stretched between the Pacific and the Atlantic coasts of Mesoamerica, while the Mayan kingdom occupied the eastern part of Mesoamerica. The Inca empire stretched 4,000 km (2,500 miles) along the west coast of South America.

Mayan pottery figurine of a powerful man

LEARNED MAYA
The Maya excelled at arithmetic and astronomy, and they used hieroglyphics, or picture writing (pp.40–41). The four Mayan books, or codices, that still exist today tell us little of their history, but deal mainly with subjects such as rituals, astronomy, and calendars.

Mayan codex

THE FOUNDING OF TENOCHTITLAN

According to their mythology, Huitzilopochtli, the tribal god of the Aztecs, promised to show his people a place where they were to settle and build their great capital, Tenochtitlan. He told them to look for an eagle perched upon a cactus with a serpent in its beak. This first page of the Codex Mendoza (a book telling the history of the Aztecs) illustrates the foundation of Tenochtitlan in either 1325 or 1345. Mexico City is built on the same site.

INCA GOLD

The Incas excelled at working metals such as silver, copper, and gold (pp.50–51). Female figures like this one have been found with Inca offerings to the gods.

Wooden beaker, or *kero*, with decoration of an Inca man holding a spear and shield

THE AZTECS

The Aztecs were a wandering tribe before they settled in the Valley of Mexico on swampy land in Lake Texcoco and founded Tenochtitlan. The city grew in size and importance until it became the capital of the mighty Aztec empire. The Aztecs conquered many peoples, demanding tribute from them (pp.26–27). Aztecs were short and stocky, with brown skin and broad faces.

Aztecs had thick, black hair

Even white teeth

Aquiline nose

Stone sculpture of Aztec head

THE ANDEAN PEOPLE

The Inca empire became the most important state in the Andean highlands in 1438, when the Incas conquered the area around the city of Cuzco and made it their capital. They went on to occupy other provinces and incorporate them into their empire. Thanks to their efficient administration system, they were able to keep control of this vast domain. The people of the Andean area were typically small, with straight, black hair and brown skin.

Almond-shaped eyes

High cheekbones

Moche pottery portrait vessel

People of Mesoamerica

MESOAMERICA IS ONE OF two areas in the Americas (the other being the central Andes) that had urban civilizations at the time of the Spanish conquest in 1519. The fact that Mesoamerican people built spectacular pyramids and temples (pp.30–31), had large markets (pp.26–27), the ball-game (pp.58–59), a sacred calendar, hieroglyphic writing (pp.40–41), several gods (pp.32–33), and practised human sacrifice (pp.36–37) sets Mesoamerica apart from its neighbours. Mesoamerican cultural history is divided into three main periods: the Preclassic or Formative, the Classic, and the Postclassic, which together stretched from about 2000 BCE until the Spanish conquest (pp.62–63). During these periods, Mesoamerica saw the rise and fall of many civilizations. In the Preclassic Period, the Olmecs were the dominant culture. The Classic Period witnessed the rise of the Teotihuacan culture and the Maya. The Postclassic Period was a time of strife and warring empires, such as those of the Toltecs and Aztecs.

WARRING AZTECS
At its height, the Aztec empire was strong and prosperous. Conquered areas were controlled by the powerful Aztec army. This illustration shows an army commander.

MAYAN RITUAL
Religion was the centre of every Mayan person's life. One of the major achievements of the Maya was the construction of superb temples and other buildings to honour their gods. These were decorated with carvings, as can be seen on this lintel showing a woman drawing blood from her tongue. Self-sacrifice was common throughout Mesoamerica.

MAP OF MESOAMERICA
Mesoamerica is both a geographical and a cultural region. At the time of the Spanish conquest, it included what is now central and southern Mexico and the peninsula of Yucatán, Guatemala, Belize, El Salvador, the westernmost part of Honduras, and a small part of Nicaragua and northern Costa Rica.

Gulf of Mexico

Yucatán Peninsula

Toltecs • *Tula*

• *Teotihuacan*

Tenochtitlan

Lake Texcoco

• *Veracruz*

Olmecs

Mixtecs

Monte Alban • **Zapotecs**

Palenque •

Chichen Itza •

Maya

Tikal •

Pacific Ocean

THE TOLTECS
The Toltec civilization, with its capital at Tula, flourished between about 900 and 1187 CE. The Toltecs were masters of architecture and the arts. They were also a great warring society, as can be seen in their many sculptures of warriors. This warrior (left) has raised arms to support an altar or shrine. The Toltecs had a great influence in Mayan territory during the Postclassic Period, and there are similarities in some of their sculptures and buildings.

THE MIXTECS
The history of the Mixtec civilization can be traced back in codices to the 7th century CE, and it existed until the time of the Spanish conquest. The Mixtecs produced superb pottery and were also very concerned with history and writing about their origins in codices (pp.40–41), many of which still survive.

The Mixtecs were famed for their pottery and designs

This type of decoration is similar to the images in Mixtec codices

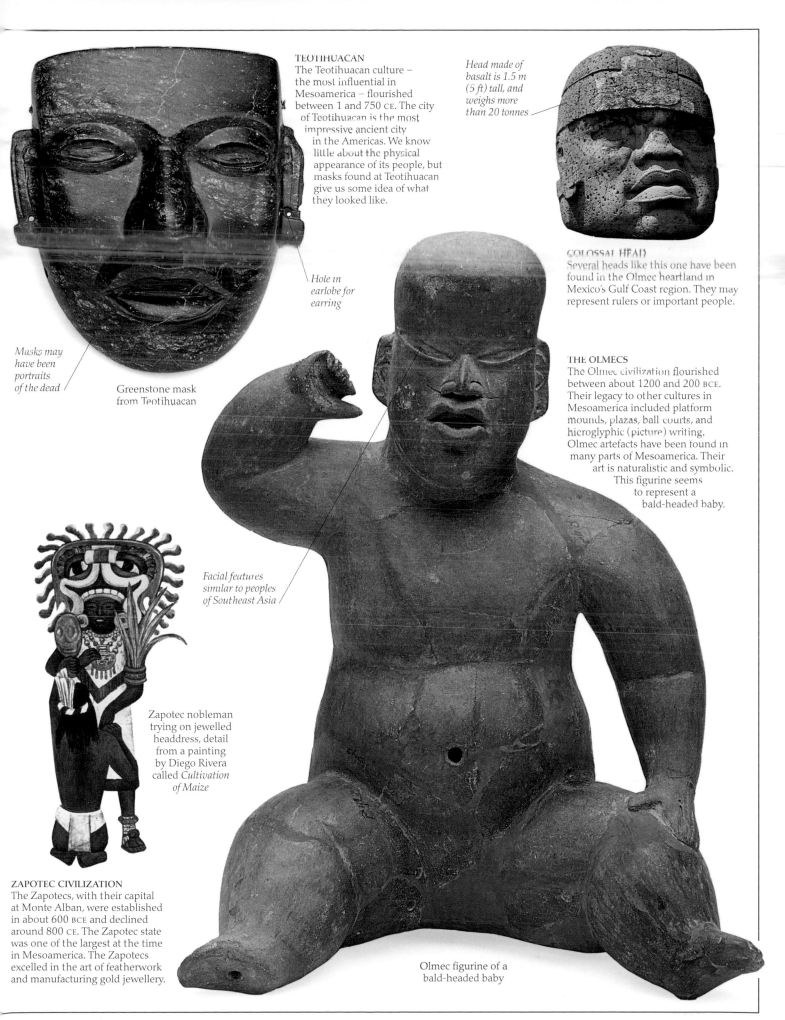

TEOTIHUACAN

The Teotihuacan culture – the most influential in Mesoamerica – flourished between 1 and 750 CE. The city of Teotihuacan is the most impressive ancient city in the Americas. We know little about the physical appearance of its people, but masks found at Teotihuacan give us some idea of what they looked like.

Hole in earlobe for earring

Masks may have been portraits of the dead

Greenstone mask from Teotihuacan

Head made of basalt is 1.5 m (5 ft) tall, and weighs more than 20 tonnes

COLOSSAL HEAD

Several heads like this one have been found in the Olmec heartland in Mexico's Gulf Coast region. They may represent rulers or important people.

THE OLMECS

The Olmec civilization flourished between about 1200 and 200 BCE. Their legacy to other cultures in Mesoamerica included platform mounds, plazas, ball courts, and hieroglyphic (picture) writing. Olmec artefacts have been found in many parts of Mesoamerica. Their art is naturalistic and symbolic. This figurine seems to represent a bald-headed baby.

Facial features similar to peoples of Southeast Asia

Zapotec nobleman trying on jewelled headdress, detail from a painting by Diego Rivera called *Cultivation of Maize*

ZAPOTEC CIVILIZATION

The Zapotecs, with their capital at Monte Alban, were established in about 600 BCE and declined around 800 CE. The Zapotec state was one of the largest at the time in Mesoamerica. The Zapotecs excelled in the art of featherwork and manufacturing gold jewellery.

Olmec figurine of a bald-headed baby

The Incas and their ancestors

BEFORE THE INCA EMPIRE reached its peak in South America, many Andean cultures had already laid the framework for its success. These cultures left no written records of their history, and all that is known of them comes from the study of their architecture, pottery, and the remains found in their graves. Archaeologists have identified separate periods of cultural growth culminating with the Incas. The first complex societies were formed in around 1800 BCE. Between this time and the rise of the Incas in the mid 15th century CE, various cultures emerged, gradually becoming highly organized civilizations with social structures, political and economic systems, specialized artisans, and a religion in which many gods were worshipped. Along the desert coast of Peru there were civilized states such as the Nazca, the Moche, and the Chimu. In the highlands, the Huari and the Tiahuanaco were complex and organized cultures. Between 1438 and 1534 CE, all of these elements were brought together and improved on under the Inca empire.

NAZCA
The Nazca inhabited the southern coastal valleys of Peru from 300 BCE to 600 CE. They were well-known for their arts, which included textiles and metalwork. But the real hallmark of the Nazca civilization is its painted pottery, decorated with realistic and mythological scenes.

INCA NOBLES
The scenes painted on vessels and other objects help us learn more about Andean life and culture. For example, Inca nobles usually carried a lance, as this painting on a wooden beaker, or *kero*, shows.

MOCHE
The Moche people flourished on the northern desert coast of Peru between about 100 CE and 700 CE. They were skilled weavers and goldsmiths, and remarkable potters. Their representations of people, plants, animals, and gods in a wide range of activities give us an insight into their lives.

Moche person of high status wearing headband with jaguar decoration and earplugs

TIAHUANACO
The Tiahuanaco empire of the Peruvian–Bolivian Altiplano (southern Peru and northwestern Bolivia) flourished between about 500 and 750 CE. It was a strong state with an impressive ceremonial centre.

Tiahuanaco pottery jaguar

HUARI
The Huari (500 to 900 CE) were neighbours of the Tiahuanaco. Their state was highly organized, with an advanced irrigation system and a distinctive architectural style. It expanded by conquering neighbouring areas. Many Huari ideas, including pottery techniques, were adopted by other Andean cultures. The Huari also had their own style of art. A common theme is an "angel" figure with wings, as seen here.

The Tiahuanaco and the Huari art styles shared many of the same symbols, especially of the cat family

THE CHANCAY

Chancay was a small kingdom that flourished from about 1000 to 1440 CE. It is named after a town on the central coast of Peru. The Chancay had unique styles of architecture and crafts, including weaving and ceramics. Chancay artisans produced a distinctive type of pottery, as can be seen from this figurine in the shape of a woman with her arms outstretched.

Eyes decorated with lines

Quito
Moche
Chimu • Cajamarca
Chan Chan
Chancay
Huari • Machu Picchu
Cuzco • Lake Titicaca
Nazca • Tiahuanaco

Pacific Ocean

THE INCA EMPIRE *(TAHUANTINSUYU)*

The Inca empire, with its capital at Cuzco, covered a large proportion of South America in the 15th and early 16th centuries. The empire stretched for 4,000 km (2,500 miles) down the west coast of South America, covering coastal desert, high mountains, and low-lying jungle. It included most of modern-day Peru, parts of Ecuador and Bolivia, northwest Argentina, and the greater part of Chile.

Gold Chimu ear ornament inlaid with semi-precious stones

Figure of Chimu warrior holding victim's head

THE CHIMU

The vast Chimu empire (1000 to 1470 CE) had a magnificent capital at Chan Chan in the same coastal area as the Moche. The Chimu were eventually conquered by the Incas. Theirs was an organized culture, with skilled architects. These gold ear ornaments are an example of the sophistication of Chimu goldsmiths.

Chancay figurine with outstretched arms

Farming

AGRICULTURE WAS A VITAL PART of life for the ancient Americans. Their farmers used sophisticated methods of cultivation, and by the time of the Spanish conquest (p.62) they were the greatest plant cultivators in the world. Maize from Mesoamerica and potatoes from the Andes (pp.24–25) were some of their contributions to the European diet. Human labour was the vital ingredient in both regions. There were no animals for carrying loads or ploughs in Mesoamerica, and although the Andean people had the llama, it could only carry very small loads. Farming methods varied according to the climate and geography of the area. The Aztecs grew their most productive crops on the *chinampas* – plots of fertile land built in swampy lakes.

GODDESS OF AGRICULTURE
This incense burner (used to burn a resin called *copal*) represents an agricultural goddess. Agricultural goddesses were often adorned with a pleated fan, like this one.

BUILDING *CHINAMPAS*
Chinampas were made by staking out narrow, rectangular strips in marshy lakes. Narrow canals were built between them for canoes to pass along. Each *chinampa* was built up with layers of thick water vegetation cut from the lake's surface and mud from the bottom of the lake. They were piled up like mats to make the plots. Willow trees were planted around the edge of each *chinampa* to make it more secure.

FERTILE PLOTS
Crops of vegetables and flowers were grown on the fertile *chinampas*, along with medicinal plants and herbs.

Maize

Rich earth from the bottom of the lake was used as fertilizer

Long, broad blade

FARMER'S TOOL
The digging stick, or *uictli*, was the essential farmer's tool. Digging sticks were used for various jobs, such as hoeing and planting.

PLANTING THE SEED
This illustration from the Florentine Codex shows an Aztec farmer planting maize using a digging stick.

DIGGING STICK
Digging sticks were made with the strongest and longest-lasting woods.

HARVEST TIME
Life in Mesoamerica and the Andean region revolved around the cycles of planting, cultivating, and harvesting crops such as maize.

MAIZE CROP
Maize was the staple food of the Maya as well as the Aztecs. It is still an important crop today.

Stone head

Wooden handle

AXE
Axes were used for chopping or hammering.

Nazca pot showing a farmer holding plants

CORNCOB VESSEL
Andean pottery was often made in the shape of the fruit and vegetables that were grown. Maize originated in Mesoamerica, but was widely grown in the Americas.

Head attached to handle with cord

HOE
This tool was used as a spade to turn the soil of the plots.

TERRACES AT MACHU PICCHU
To get the highest yield from their crops, the Incas used sophisticated terracing and irrigation methods on hillsides in the highlands. Building terraces meant that they could use more land for cultivation, and also helped to resist erosion of the land by wind and rain.

TENDING CROPS
In the Andean region, cultivating the soil was the basis of life. Farmers tended their crops using simple tools such as a digging stick, a clod breaker, and a hoe.

Hunting and fishing

JADE FISH
People from coastal regions drew inspiration from fish and marine life to decorate pottery and jade objects.

HUNTING AND FISHING were important activities in Mesoamerica and in the Andean regions. Meat and fish were part of the diet, especially in the Andean region, depending on what was available in the area. Animal life in the Andes was most abundant in the high mountains of the north, where large mammals such as deer and vicuñas (wild relatives of the llama) roamed. In Mesoamerica, the largest animals were the peccary (a relative of the pig) and the deer, which were hunted with bows and arrows. Dogs, rabbits, and other small animals were also eaten. Mesoamericans and South Americans fished for everything from shellfish to large fish and sea mammals using nets, harpoons, and angling. They made fishing hooks from sturdy cactus thorns, shell, and bone. Hooks were also made of copper in South America.

IN THE NET
Catching waterfowl in nets was widespread in Mesoamerica's lake areas.

FISHING NET
The lake system in and around Tenochtitlan provided people with fish and waterfowl, fresh water for drinking, and irrigation for crops. Sometimes fish were transported in canoes to markets and sold. Many nets in present-day Mexico are similar to those produced by the Aztecs and other Mesoamerican peoples. The most common net used by the Aztecs was bag-shaped, like this one, and made of fibres from the agave plant.

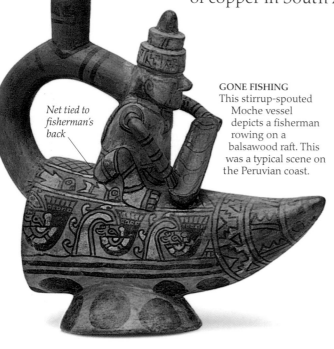

Net tied to fisherman's back

GONE FISHING
This stirrup-spouted Moche vessel depicts a fisherman rowing on a balsawood raft. This was a typical scene on the Peruvian coast.

FAMILY TRADITION
Many trades, such as fishing, were passed from father to son. Boys were taught to fish when very young, and at the age of 14 they went out fishing alone.

Raft is made from woven reeds – the Aztecs and Maya made their canoes from hollowed-out tree trunks

REED RAFT
Watercraft were fashioned from reeds because of the shortage of wood in areas where few or no trees grew. This type of raft was – and still is – used high in the Andes around Lake Titicaca and also on the coast. Large rafts between 4.5 m and 6.1 m (14 ft 6 in and 20 ft) long were equipped with a wooden mast for raising and lowering the sail made of reeds.

DEER-HUNTING SCENE
This beautiful Mayan plate from Yucatán, decorated with black and bright orange paints, shows a lively hunting scene. The hunter at the centre has already captured a deer, which he carries draped over his head and back. Surrounding this central image are other hunters wearing deer masks in an attempt to distract the animal they want to catch.

Hunter carrying deer

Hunter disguised as prey

FATAL WEAPON
Slings were used as long-range weapons by both Inca hunters and soldiers. They were made from plaited llama wool. The stone was placed in a small cradle. Holding both ends, the sling was whirled around the head. Releasing one end sent the stone hurtling towards its target with great accuracy. The injury inflicted by the stone could be fatal.

Stone placed in plaited woollen cradle

A BIRD IN THE HAND
The art of the ancient South American people shows us what their activities were. This wooden cup is painted with a scene of a man hunting birds.

BOW AND ARROW *right*
Bows, arrows, and spear throwers (below) were weapons used originally in Central Mexico, and later introduced to the Mayan area. Along with the javelin and the sling, the bow and arrow were used for hunting animals at long range.

Bow

SHOOTING FISH
The Maya caught fish in lagoons using bows and arrows.

Arrow

Arrow head made from obsidian

Spear

NAZCA FOX
This fox was part of the decoration on a Nazca pot. Foxes usually symbolized war. They were also considered pests and were killed mainly with clubs.

SPEAR AND SPEAR THROWER
Spears (above) had a fire-hardened tip or a point made of chipped stone or obsidian. They were propelled by a spear thrower, or *atlatl* (below). This was a long piece of wood with a groove down the centre.

Spear thrower

Finger holes for gripping spear thrower

The shaft of the spear rested in this groove

Mesoamerican cities

THE PEOPLES OF MESOAMERICA established their cities in a variety of geographic and climatic areas. Some were located in the highlands, others in jungles or coastal regions. The Olmecs built their cities in tropical regions, while the people of Teotihuacan, the Toltecs, and the Aztecs founded theirs in the highlands. Mayan cities were set up in both highland and lowland regions. These geographical differences influenced the architecture of the cities. As time passed, the cities grew in size. The Olmecs (1200 BC) lived in small cities, but Teotihuacan (200 CE) had an estimated 150,000 inhabitants or more. The central areas of Mesoamerican cities were reserved for religious and public buildings, and for the houses of rulers and of the elite. The homes of ordinary people were built outside these areas.

CHICHEN ITZA
The Mayan city of Chichen Itza was built at a strategic location in the centre of the Yucatán Peninsula. Chichen Itza grew into an important commercial centre that maintained links with many other areas. It is thought that the Toltecs of highland Central Mexico later established themselves at Chichen Itza.

Temple-pyramid *El Castillo* (The Castle) at Chichen Itza

TRIBUTE TOWNS
The Codex Mendoza (p.7) gives the names of towns that paid tribute to Tenochtitlan, as well as the goods required. Each of these glyphs (left) represents the name of a subject town.

PALENQUE
This Mayan temple is situated in Palenque, in the midst of tropical jungle. Hidden in the pyramid was the funeral chamber of Lord Pacal (p.53), who ruled for 68 years and was buried in this magnificent resting place in 683 CE. His sarcophagus (stone coffin) contained some of the most beautiful jade objects ever found in Mesoamerica.

Temple of the Inscriptions at Palenque

Shrine to Tlaloc, god of rain

Great Temple of the Aztecs

Temple steps

Pyramid of the Moon

Avenue of the Dead

Pyramid of the Sun

Rio de San Juan

TEOTIHUACAN STYLE
Many of the structures at Teotihuacan were built in the same style. They consisted of a sloping base with a flat rectangular top. This architectural feature is also found in some Mayan cities, such as at Tikal in Guatemala.

MAP OF TEOTIHUACAN
This plan of Teotihuacan's ceremonial centre shows its main axis, the Avenue of the Dead. The city's two most imposing structures are the Pyramid of the Sun and the Pyramid of the Moon. Originally, all the buildings at Teotihuacan were painted, some with mythological scenes.

TOLTEC WARRIOR
This is one of the warriors on the top of Temple B at Tula. These warriors once supported a roof. The warrior is equipped with a spear thrower, and his breastplate in the shape of a butterfly indicates that he is a warrior.

Temple B, or the Temple of Quetzalcoatl, at Tula

TULA
The Toltec capital of Tula reflects the beginning of an era of great military action. Despite Tula being the capital of the god Quetzalcoatl, who was opposed to war and human sacrifice, there are carvings of warriors equipped for war everywhere, including on top of temple pyramids.

Shrine of Huitzilopochtli, god of war

Map of Tenochtitlan

Skulls of sacrificed victims

Brazier

TENOCHTITLAN
This European map (left) shows Tenochtitlan, the physical and spiritual heart of the Aztec empire. The city was built on a lake and was reached by causeways, or raised roads. The Spanish conquerors, or *conquistadores*, described the streets as being large, wide, and straight. The Great Temple of the Aztecs (pp.30–31) was at the city's centre. The model below shows the Great Temple inside the sacred precinct. It had shrines to both Tlaloc, god of rain, and Huitzilopochtli, god of war, who was also the god of the Aztecs. Just outside the ceremonial centre there were palaces, warrior schools, shrines, and a ball-court (pp.58–59).

Cities of the Andes

THE PEOPLE OF THE ANDEAN REGION lived either in highland or coastal areas. They built their cities to suit the location, using materials that were locally available. Typical highland buildings had sloping, thatched roofs and masonry walls. Buildings on the coast tended to have flat roofs and mud-brick (adobe) walls covered by painted mud plaster. Highland cities, such as Machu Picchu, could not be built on a regular grid plan like Chan Chan and other cities in flat, coastal areas. The first buildings to be lived in as homes date back to the 4th century BCE. Government buildings, storehouses, bridges, canals, and other public constructions were built by ordinary people as a kind of labour tax, with the state providing the necessary materials.

INCA MASONS
The Incas are renowned for their fine stonework. Masons cut huge, stone bricks using just a stone hammer and then polished them with wet sand. The bricks fitted so closely together that no mortar was needed.

TIAHUANACO
The city of Tiahuanaco (p.10) is situated on a high plain nearly 4,000 m (13,100 ft) above sea level and rimmed by the Andes mountains. The stunning architecture of its ceremonial centre included an impressive number of stone sculptures. The Gateway of the Sun (above) was carved from a single block of stone. A carving over the doorway portrays a Sun god.

OLLANTAYTAMBO
The Inca town of Ollantaytambo has some of Peru's most impressive architectural remains. This doorway is made of rectangular stone blocks, each precisely cut and fitted to a specific position.

Bird motif on adobe wall of royal compound, Chan Chan

Royal compound at Chan Chan, capital of the Chimu kingdom

ADOBE DECORATION
The Chimu decorated their thick adobe (mud) walls with moulded motifs, usually associated with the sea, such as birds, fish, and men in boats.

CHAN CHAN
The Chimu people built proper urban centres, and Chan Chan, the coastal capital of the Chimu empire, is a good example of this. The city was organized on a grid plan, and covered approximately 6 sq km (2.3 sq miles). It contained 10 compounds, each enclosed by a high adobe wall. These are thought to be the royal residences and administrative centres of the Chimu kings. Each king lived, died, and was buried in his own secluded compound.

European
map of
Cuzco

CUZCO

Encircled by high
peaks, Cuzco – the religious and political capital of the Incas – is
situated at the heart of the Andes. The town was divided into sections
by narrow paved streets, designed to represent the four quarters of
the Inca empire. It had ceremonial plazas, palaces, and temples. Only
the rulers and nobility lived in the city centre. This European drawing
wrongly portrays Cuzco as a walled town. Much of the city was
destroyed by the Spanish, who built their own city on the Inca ruins.

Stone walls of
Sacsahuaman
fort

SACSAHUAMAN FORT

Cuzco was protected from the enemy by the fortress of
Sacsahuaman, built on a steep hill overlooking the city from the
north. The fort was constructed with locally quarried stone, and
each giant block was individually shaped. These three impressive
stone walls, which stand 16 m (52 ft) high, guarded the fortress.

INCA BATHS

Inca palaces sometimes had
sunken stone baths in which
the kings could relax and
bathe. Water ran along stone
channels into the baths. These
baths at Tambomachay, near
Cuzco, were built at the site of
a sacred spring. They were
used by the Inca kings.

Inca baths at Tambomachay

Machu Picchu

MACHU PICCHU

Strategically positioned at the edge of the Inca empire, the remote city of Machu Picchu
was probably built in the mid to late 15th century. The Spanish *conquistadores* never
found Machu Picchu, and the city was not discovered until 1911. The site is an
outstanding example of Inca architecture – a natural fortress protected by steep
slopes, surrounded by high mountain peaks, and approached from only one
direction. Of its 143 granite buildings, about 80 were houses and
the rest were ceremonial buildings such as temples.
Many mummies were found at Machu
Picchu, most of them women.

Family life

COUPLE EMBRACING
In both Mesoamerica and the Andean region, a wife's role was to obey her husband. Even in art, women were often depicted in a passive stance, and men in a more active position. This Mayan pottery statue shows a man embracing a woman. Both wear elaborate headdresses, ear plugs, and necklaces indicating that the they were a wealthy couple.

Figure has eyes and teeth inlaid with shell

THE MESOAMERICAN MAN, as a husband and father, was responsible for the well-being of his household. He was expected to support his family, as well as his government, through hard work and by paying taxes. The woman, as a wife and mother, devoted her time and energy to running her household and caring for her children. Girls were taught domestic chores, such as weaving and cooking, and sons followed their fathers while they worked. Children had free schooling, and nobles had their own schools. Family life was similar in the Andean region. The father worked to support the family and pay taxes; the mother worked in the home, helped her husband with his work, and cared for the children. Inca commoners had to educate their own children.

Aztec couple during marriage ceremony

JUST MARRIED
One of the rituals in an Aztec wedding ceremony was to tie the young man's cloak and the girl's blouse together. The wedding party took place afterwards, with dancing and singing.

FERTILE BLESSING
Both the Mesoamericans and the Incas considered it important for a married couple to have children. The Aztecs worshipped goddesses of fertility. This wooden Aztec sculpture is of a young woman dressed in a skirt and bare-breasted. She may be a goddess of fertility.

CELEBRATION
There were great celebrations when an Aztec baby was born. The festivities lasted for days, during which astrologers checked to see when would be a favourable day for the baby to be named.

Stirrup handle

Two helpers aid a woman giving birth

CHILDBIRTH SCENE
The Aztecs did not have midwives. When giving birth, Andean women were helped by women who had given birth to twins, and also by their neighbours. After the birth, the mother washed herself and her baby in the river. The umbilical cord was not thrown away, but was kept in the house.

BRINGING UP BABIES
Family scenes are common in Aztec art and show women performing various activities. This woman is carrying two children, one under each arm. One of the main roles of an Aztec woman was to bring up her children until they were ready to leave home and marry.

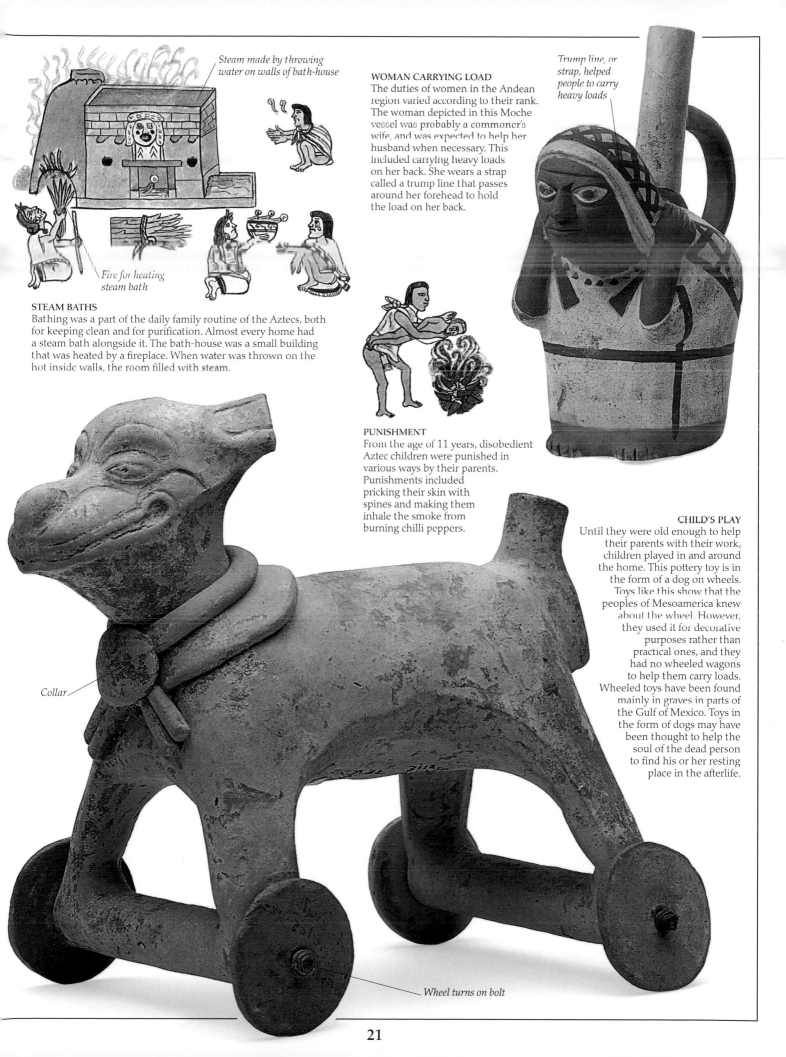

Steam made by throwing water on walls of bath-house

Fire for heating steam bath

STEAM BATHS
Bathing was a part of the daily family routine of the Aztecs, both for keeping clean and for purification. Almost every home had a steam bath alongside it. The bath-house was a small building that was heated by a fireplace. When water was thrown on the hot inside walls, the room filled with steam.

WOMAN CARRYING LOAD
The duties of women in the Andean region varied according to their rank. The woman depicted in this Moche vessel was probably a commoner's wife, and was expected to help her husband when necessary. This included carrying heavy loads on her back. She wears a strap called a trump line that passes around her forehead to hold the load on her back.

Trump line, or strap, helped people to carry heavy loads

PUNISHMENT
From the age of 11 years, disobedient Aztec children were punished in various ways by their parents. Punishments included pricking their skin with spines and making them inhale the smoke from burning chilli peppers.

CHILD'S PLAY
Until they were old enough to help their parents with their work, children played in and around the home. This pottery toy is in the form of a dog on wheels. Toys like this show that the peoples of Mesoamerica knew about the wheel. However, they used it for decorative purposes rather than practical ones, and they had no wheeled wagons to help them carry loads. Wheeled toys have been found mainly in graves in parts of the Gulf of Mexico. Toys in the form of dogs may have been thought to help the soul of the dead person to find his or her resting place in the afterlife.

Collar

Wheel turns on bolt

At home

WATER GOURD
The gourd, a vegetable with a hard shell, was frequently made into a container after being dried out. Gourds were mainly used for carrying water. This type of gourd grows in most parts of the Americas.

Maize cob used as cork

Sharp, wooden teeth

HANDY TOOL
Combs were made of bone or wood. They were used for hairdressing and, in South America, for preparing wool. Some were even used to make patterns on pottery.

THE AZTECS, MAYA, AND INCAS lived in simple houses, often containing only one main room and very little in the way of furniture. Inca houses were made of stone bricks or of mud (adobe), while most Aztec and Mayan houses were made of adobe. For the Aztecs, furniture consisted of just a few beds made of reed mats, low tables, and reed chests for clothes. The Aztec home had an inner courtyard with a kitchen, and a small shrine to the gods. The bathroom was in a separate building. The homes of wealthy nobles and dignitaries had more rooms, more elaborate furniture, and bigger gardens.

INSIDE AN AZTEC HOUSE
An Aztec woman's home meant almost everything to her. She spent most of her day in the house, looking after the children, cooking, or weaving.

MULTIPURPOSE POT
This pot was used to store liquids and food. It was stood on a ring made of reeds to keep it upright.

REED MAT
Mesoamerican people sat, played, and slept on reed mats. This type of mat would have been used as a rug on the floor of most houses. Other, thicker mats were used as beds. Both rich and poor homes had mats like the one above.

Bowl has three sturdy legs

TRIPOD BOWL
Potters working in Teotihuacan often made three-legged bowls like this, sometimes with a lid. Pots for day-to-day use were usually plain, but others had a pattern, either cut into the surface or painted on, as here.

INCA HOUSE
The most common type of Inca house, whether made from adobe or stone, was rectangular with a thatched roof, and usually had just one room. There was no furniture in an Inca house. The stone blocks used to build houses were carved so that that they fitted together perfectly, and there was no need for cement.

Inca doors and windows were shaped like a trapezium – four-sided, but with only two parallel sides

CURVED KNIFE
Knives with metal blades of various shapes were known as *tumi*. This Peruvian *tumi* is made of copper with a fitted bone handle.

Curved blade may have been used for cutting up food

End of handle is in the shape of an animal's head

Chisel has a wooden handle carved in the shape of a jaguar

HOW PEOPLE LIVED
This pot was found in an ancient Peruvian grave. It is an elaborate, decorated version of the type of pot that would have been used in the Andean region for everyday cooking and eating. Objects found in graves give us an idea of how people lived long ago.

JAGUAR CHISEL
Everyday Andean tools, such as this chisel, have been found in sacred places, or *huacas*.

GRINDING STONE
Early every morning, the women would revive the hearth fire and grind maize on the grinding stone, or *metlatl* (made of volcanic stone, usually basalt). Grinding stones were basic tools in the kitchen. Today, grinding stones are still used throughout the Mesoamerican region, mainly for grinding maize into flour.

Cylindrical stone used to press the maize against the grinding stone

Vessels with stirrup spouts such as this one were made only in South America

Water pot in the shape of a Moche building

HIGH-CLASS VESSEL
In the Andean region, a person's status could be told by the kind of drinking vessel he or she used. Peasants drank from gourd bowls, while the well-to-do drank from pottery containers like the one shown here. Some wealthy people drank from gold or silver vessels.

23

Food and drink

THE MESOAMERICANS AND ANDEANS ate simply. Maize (corn) was the central food in their diet, along with vegetables such as beans and squashes. Not all foods were grown in both regions, however. Potatoes and quinoa (a grain) came from the Andean region, while avocados and tomatoes were mainly consumed in Mesoamerica, along with a wide variety of fruit. Maize was made into a sort of porridge, called *atole* in Mesoamerica and *capia* in Inca territory. Maize cakes were eaten in both regions, but only the Mesoamerican peoples ate maize pancakes known as *tortillas* with every meal. A favourite dish among the Aztecs and Incas was *tamales*, a kind of envelope of steamed maize stuffed with vegetables or meat. In both Mesoamerica and the Andean region, it was customary for people to eat twice a day; the Mesoamericans ate their main meal during the hottest part of the day.

Guinea pig meat was the only meat regularly eaten by the Andeans.

Cocoa beans

Chocolate was made with ground cocoa beans and water

COCOA
A chocolate drink made from cocoa was drunk by wealthy Mesoamericans. It was sweetened with honey and flavoured with vanilla.

Cocoa pod

Bowl-shaped stone mortar

Club-shaped pestle

MORTAR AND PESTLE
Chillies and tomatoes were used for making sauces. They were crushed with a stone called a pestle in a mortar, which was a stone bowl that stood on three small feet.

Comal

TORTILLAS
The Mesoamerican diet is still centred around *tortillas*. Once the *tortillas* have been made, they are cooked over the fire on a pottery disc called a *comal*.

WOMEN PREPARING MAIZE
The preparation of maize was a daily task for Mesoamerican women. This section of a painting by the Mexican artist Diego Rivera shows a woman grinding corn kernels into flour between a stone roller and slab. The flour is made into a dough, which another woman pats into *tortillas*.

LLAMA
The tender meat of the llama was eaten by the Incas and their ancestors. However, they ate it with moderation, since the llama was useful as a pack animal and it also provided wool for textiles.

Llama tied up with ropes

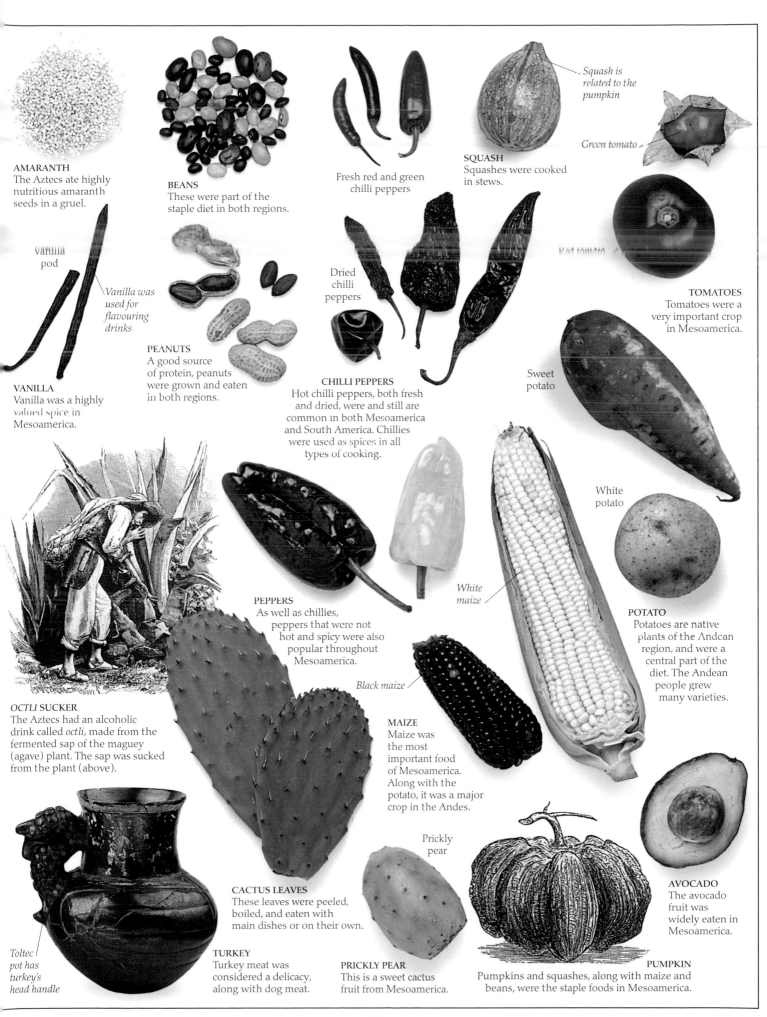

AMARANTH
The Aztecs ate highly nutritious amaranth seeds in a gruel.

BEANS
These were part of the staple diet in both regions.

Fresh red and green chilli peppers

Squash is related to the pumpkin

SQUASH
Squashes were cooked in stews.

Green tomato

Vanilla pod

Vanilla was used for flavouring drinks

PEANUTS
A good source of protein, peanuts were grown and eaten in both regions.

Dried chilli peppers

Red tomato

TOMATOES
Tomatoes were a very important crop in Mesoamerica.

VANILLA
Vanilla was a highly valued spice in Mesoamerica.

CHILLI PEPPERS
Hot chilli peppers, both fresh and dried, were and still are common in both Mesoamerica and South America. Chillies were used as spices in all types of cooking.

Sweet potato

White potato

White maize

Black maize

PEPPERS
As well as chillies, peppers that were not hot and spicy were also popular throughout Mesoamerica.

POTATO
Potatoes are native plants of the Andean region, and were a central part of the diet. The Andean people grew many varieties.

OCTLI SUCKER
The Aztecs had an alcoholic drink called *octli*, made from the fermented sap of the maguey (agave) plant. The sap was sucked from the plant (above).

MAIZE
Maize was the most important food of Mesoamerica. Along with the potato, it was a major crop in the Andes.

Prickly pear

Toltec pot has turkey's head handle

CACTUS LEAVES
These leaves were peeled, boiled, and eaten with main dishes or on their own.

TURKEY
Turkey meat was considered a delicacy, along with dog meat.

PRICKLY PEAR
This is a sweet cactus fruit from Mesoamerica.

AVOCADO
The avocado fruit was widely eaten in Mesoamerica.

PUMPKIN
Pumpkins and squashes, along with maize and beans, were the staple foods in Mesoamerica.

Trade and tribute

CODEX TRIBUTE
As well as dealing with history and daily life, the Aztec Codex Mendoza records details of tributes paid.

400 gourd bowls

400 simply decorated cotton blankets

400 heavily decorated cotton blankets

8,000 bundles of *copal* incense

60 jars of honey

2 bins, 1 of maize and 1 of chia seeds

IN MESOAMERICA and in the Andean region, it was the commoners who mainly supported the state by paying taxes. People of high rank did not pay taxes, nor did the sick and those with disabilities. In Inca territory, each province had to pay specific amounts of tribute to the government. At Tenochtitlan, the Aztec capital, the residents of each borough belonged to an institution called a *calpulli*, whose leader made sure that taxes were paid. Goods of all kinds were exchanged in both regions, and in Mesoamerica all the products of the land were sold in splendid marketplaces. Aztec merchants went on long expeditions to distant lands to trade for such items as tropical feathers, gold, fine stones, and jaguar skins.

RUNNER
This Moche pot depicts a runner. Runners, or *chasquis*, ran from one place to the next, usually carrying messages. The Incas had an excellent road system that was essential for controlling the empire, for trade, and for communication.

Jaguar headdress

Jaguar warrior's suit

Feather shield

WARRIOR'S SUIT AND SHIELD
Tunics and shields were very expensive items of tribute. Tunics were either made of feather-covered material or of animal pelts. The jaguar headdress (left) was one of the warrior's insignia and also a symbol of power. According to the Codex Mendoza, tribute of this kind had to be paid once a year.

THE SALE OF MAIZE
Much can be learned from the murals of Diego Rivera about how the ancient Mexicans lived. Rivera, one of the most remarkable modern Mexican muralists, was well-read about life in Tenochtitlan. This detail of a busy market scene shows women selling various types of maize.

FUR TRADE
Animal skins were sold in the market at Tlatelolco. The skin of the puma was particularly valued by the Maya, because its tawny colour reminded them of the Sun. Jaguar skins were equally valued. Their black spots were thought to symbolize the night sky. Jaguar skins were used as seats for the rulers, and as book covers. They were also worn as cloaks.

Ocelot skin

Puma skin

Jaguar skin

TLATELOLCO MARKET
When the Spanish arrived in Mexico, they found that the market at Tlatelolco (the sister city of Tenochtitlan) was bigger and better stocked than any market in Spain. Supervisors regulated prices, and judges were present in case of disputes or theft. Much of the buying and selling was done by barter – exchanging products – although copper axes sometimes served as money in both Mesoamerica and in the Andes.

Cocoa beans

Mamey seeds

Axe heads

Quetzal feather

Jade beads

Tropical bird feather

TRADING
Items such as cocoa beans and feathers were in great demand, as vast quantities of each were paid in tribute. The merchants from Tenochtitlan and neighbouring major cities exported and traded luxury objects made from imported raw materials or materials obtained by tribute. In return for their wares, they obtained goods such as tropical feathers (especially quetzal feathers), cocoa beans, animal skins, and gold.

Recording storehouse goods on a quipu

Storing agricultural produce in government granaries

INCA STOREHOUSES *left*
The Incas stockpiled goods such as cloth, maize, wool, potatoes, and weapons in storehouses. These supplies could be used by government officials and those who were in need due to an illness. They could also be distributed after a crisis or a siege.

Simply decorated pottery vessel for everyday use

All the pottery stalls were placed together in the market

Simple pottery bowl

People met at the market to exchange news as well as goods

The warrior

WARFARE was a normal part of life in both Mesoamerica and the Inca region of South America, and city-states frequently fought each other. In Mesoamerica, youths had to join the army at the age of 17 for a period of intensive training. The Inca and Mesoamerican peoples were educated in the arts of war, and the fighting spirit was encouraged. Among the Aztecs, the best and most common way to climb the social ladder was by showing courage in battle. One of the main aims of going to war was to capture enemy warriors for sacrifice. Aztec warriors were in a constant "sacred war", as they believed that human sacrifice kept the Sun in motion (pp.36–37). Both the Incas and the Aztecs added newly conquered areas to their empires. As power and wealth grew, they developed a thirst for more conquests that would enrich the state and add to the glory of the emperor.

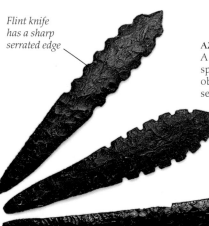

TOLTEC WARRIOR
This sculpture shows a richly attired Toltec warrior wearing a feather headdress, ear plugs, and a butterfly breastplate. In one hand he carries an *atlatl*, or spear thrower, and in the other a sheaf of darts.

CAPTURED
For taking captives, Aztec warriors were awarded costumes with distinctive designs, such as jaguar costumes and mantles. The more captives a warrior took, the more elaborate his costume.

Flint knife has a sharp serrated edge

AZTEC WEAPONS
A warrior usually carried one or two throwing spears. They were made of wood and edged with obsidian – a volcanic glass that is sharp enough to sever a horse's head – or a type of stone called chert. He also had a wooden *macuahuitl*, or war club, edged with obsidian. As well a club and spears, warriors carried stabbing javelins and round shields with protective feather fringes. Flint and obsidian knives (left) were also used for human sacrifices.

Club

Long, razor-sharp knife made from obsidian

WAR CLUB
The *macuahuitl*, or war club, was about 76 cm (30 in) long. It had grooved sides set with sharp obsidian blades.

EFFIGY POT
The Moche culture from the north coast of Peru often depicted warriors on pottery vessels, such as this warrior holding a club. Shields were often shown strapped to the wrists.

THROWING SPEAR
The flakes of sharp obsidian stone around the head of a wooden throwing spear were capable of inflicting deep cuts.

Obsidian blades around head of spear

STONE OF MOCTEZUMA I
This large, round stone depicts the battles of the Aztec ruler Moctezuma I. The detail shown here symbolizes the capture of a city and its incorporation into the Aztec empire. The top of the stone was used for gladiatorial fights. It has a hole in the centre, which acted as a vessel for the hearts of sacrificial victims and other offerings.

TERRACOTTA EAGLE WARRIOR
The most prestigious military orders were those of the eagle and the jaguar, each of which had its own special warrior costume. This life-size sculpture represents an eagle warrior. It is one of a pair that was found flanking a doorway to the chamber where the eagle warriors met, next to the Great Temple of the Aztecs in Tenochtitlan. The eagle was the symbol of the Sun, to whom all sacrifices were offered.

Helmet shaped like an eagle's beak

The Aztec warrior
The ideal Aztec warrior was noble, brave, and had to serve and respect the gods. Warriors were so important in Aztec Mexico that the Aztec ruler had to start his reign on the battlefield, adding cities and provinces to the empire, and capturing prisoners for ritual sacrifice – an essential part of the Aztec religion.

The eagle warrior's costume has wings on the arms, to imitate the eagle

Imitation talons

FEATHER SHIELD
All Aztec warriors carried a shield for protection. This one is made of jaguar skin and brightly coloured tropical feathers. Featherworkers were responsible for making shields, headdresses, fans, and other objects. Some of these were made of turkey and duck feathers, but many of the most valuable objects were made of bright green quetzal feathers.

TEMPLE WARRIOR
This watercolour painting of a warrior figure decorated the doorway of a temple in the Mayan city of Chichen Itza. The warrior is dressed and armed in a similar fashion to a Toltec warrior, as Toltec influence was great in some Mayan territories. He wears a shield around his waist, protective bands on one arm and on his legs, and is carrying spears.

Religious life

R**ELIGION TOUCHED** almost every aspect of Mesoamerican and Inca life. One of the many focal points for their religious rites were sacred buildings, or temples, dedicated to their gods. In the Andean region, everyone worshipped a variety of shrines and objects and the natural forces associated with them, known as *huacas*. The Aztecs also worshipped sacred places. Within the official Inca state religion the Sun was the most important god. It was a dominant force and a symbol of prestige and power. The Incas worshipped the Sun mainly so that they would have abundant crops. The Aztec religion was also concerned with the Sun. The Aztecs believed that they lived in the era of the fifth Sun and that one day the world would end violently. In order to postpone their destruction, men performed human sacrifices. Their duty was to feed the gods with human blood, thereby keeping the Sun alive.

Codex illustration of an Aztec temple at Tenochtitlan

TEMPLE OF THE GIANT JAGUAR
To worship their gods, the Maya built magnificent ceremonial centres filled with temples, courts, and plazas. This majestic temple stands in the ceremonial centre of the Mayan city of Tikal. Also known as Temple I, it is the funerary pyramid of the Mayan ruler Hasaw Chan K'awil. It has nine sloping terraces and is topped by a huge ornamental structure called a roof comb.

Intihuatana stone pointed directly at the Sun on the winter solstice

SOLSTICE STONE
Throughout their empire, the Incas built temples for the cult of the Sun. The Intihuatana stone at Machu Picchu worked as a solar clock. It allowed people to calculate the winter solstice for the important festival of the Sun god. Intihuatana means "hitching post of the Sun".

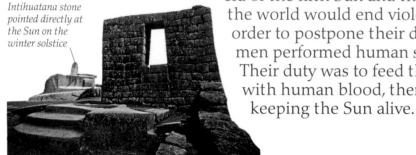

Priests performing rituals in New Fire ceremony

AZTEC NEW FIRE CEREMONY
This religious event took place in temples every 52 years. When the day arrived, people extinguished all fires and discarded idols and household utensils. The new century began when the Sun's rays appeared again at dawn.

Bodies of sacrificial victims thrown down stairs after sacrifice

MODEL OF THE GREAT TEMPLE AT TENOCHTITLAN
At the heart of the city of Tenochtitlan was a walled precinct. Within it, sharing a single tall pyramid, were the twin shrines to Tlaloc, the god of rain, and Huitzilopochtli, the god of war and the tribal god of the Aztecs. The Great Temple was the physical and symbolic centre of the Aztec world, where human sacrifices and offerings to the gods took place. Each Aztec ruler tried to make a bigger and more impressive new temple. This model shows the many temples that were built, one above the other. The oldest, inner temple has a *chacmool* (a sculpture with a receptacle for hearts and blood) on the left and a sacrificial stone on the right. The excavators of the site found more than 6,000 objects buried as offerings to Tlaloc and Huitzilopochtli.

Shrine to
Tlaloc, god
of rain

Chacmool

Shrine to Huitzilopochtli, god of war

Sacrificial
stone

SKULL PANEL
Real skulls were placed
outside temples in skull racks,
known in the Aztec language
of Nahuatl as *tzompantli*.
This panel of skulls is from
the Great Temple of the
Aztecs. The skulls were
usually those of people
sacrificed to the gods.

Snake's head
protruding from wall

Sculpture still
has traces of its
original paintwork

RECLINING FIGURE
This *chacmool* was found at the entrance
of the shrine to Tlaloc at the summit of the
Great Temple of Tenochtitlan. He holds a
container for the hearts and blood of people
sacrificed to the gods of rain and agriculture.

Gods and goddesses

Yacatecuhtli, Aztec god of merchants and travellers

T<small>HE MESOAMERICAN</small> and Inca peoples worshipped many gods. They had similar religions – based on the worship of mainly agricultural gods – even though the gods' names and the symbols for them were different. People asked their gods for good crops and good health. The main Inca god was the creator god Viracocha. His assistants were the gods of the Sun, Moon, stars, and thunder, as well as the gods of the earth and the sea. As farming occupied such an important place in both regions, the "earth mother", or earth goddess, was particularly important. As with Inca deities, many Aztec gods were connected with nature or natural forces, but the Aztecs also had other gods, including gods of war, hunting, and merchants.

Xipe Totec wearing the skin of a sacrificial victim

RAIN GOD
Many Mesoamerican vessels and sculptures are associated with Tlaloc, the god of rain and agricultural fertility. It is likely that this water vessel depicts the face of the god of rain, as it contains the vital liquid necessary to fertilize the earth.

Tlaloc had "goggle eyes"

GOD OF THE SPRINGTIME
The Aztec god of the springtime and of vegetation was called Xipe Totec ("Our Flayed Lord"). He was also the patron of metal workers. The victims sacrificed in honour of this god were flayed (skinned alive). After flaying the victim, priests would wear his skin. This symbolized the annual spring renewal of vegetation – in other words the renewal of the earth's "skin".

Xipe Totec, god of springtime and of vegetation

Quetzalcoatl, the feathered serpent   *Tlaloc, the rain god*   Reconstruction of temple of Quetzalcoatl in Teotihuacan

GOD OF NATURE
Quetzalcoatl, whose name means "feathered serpent", was a god of nature – of the air and the earth. The temple of Quetzalcoatl at Teotihuacan is decorated with large sculptures of feathered serpents, as this reconstruction shows.

Chicomecoatl wore a rectangular headdress with pleated rosettes at the corners

AZTEC MAIZE GODDESS

Three goddesses were associated with maize. This statue depicts Chicomecoatl, the goddess of mature maize. This was the best seed-corn of the harvest, which was put away for sowing. There was also a goddess of tender maize and another who was the personification of the maize plant.

Double maize cob

The Incas worshipped the Moon and the Sun

WAR GOD

Huitzilopochtli ("The Hummingbird of the Left") was the tribal god of the Aztecs. This illustration shows him armed with his serpent of fire and his shield.

GOD OF THE DEAD

Mictlantecuhtli was god of the dead in Aztec Mexico. Those who died a natural death went to Mictlan, the place where he lived, in the cold and infernal region of the fleshless.

SEPTEMBER FESTIVAL

The Incas celebrated different religious festivities each month of the year. Here we see the celebrations for September, which were dedicated to female goddesses. This festivity was celebrated under the protection of the Moon and the Sun gods.

WORSHIPPING THE SUN

Worship of Inti, the Sun god, was pivotal to Inca religion. Both Aztecs and Incas worshipped the Sun and the earth, Mamachocha ("Mother of the lakes and sea"), which are both essential for good harvests. The Sun was the most important god of the Inca royal dynasty. Inca kings believed that they were descendants of Inti.

Gold disc

Ceremonial urn depicting Chac with a bowl in his right hand and a ball of smoking incense in his left

SKY OR MOON GOD

The handle of this Peruvian ceremonial knife is decorated with the image of either the sky or the Moon god. His arms are opened wide, and he is holding two discs. He wears a beautiful filigree headdress with turquoise inlay.

Turquoise was used for the inlays of the eyes, necklace, ear plugs, and the clothing

Ornate ceremonial knife handle

MAYAN GOD OF RAIN

The Mayan god of rain was called Chac. One of the sacrifices in honour of this god was to drown children in wells. In some regions, the god of rain was so important that the facades of buildings were covered with masks of Chac.

Life after death

THE PEOPLE OF Mesoamerica and South America believed that, after they died, they would carry on living in another world. They were buried with all kinds of things that might prove useful to them in the afterlife. By studying the goods found in graves, pre-Hispanic codices, and early colonial manuscripts, archaeologists have pieced together some of their beliefs about death and the afterlife. It was the way the Aztecs died, rather than the way they lived, that decided what would happen to them in the afterlife. If a person died a normal death, his or her soul had to pass through the nine levels of the underworld before reaching Mictlan, the realm of the god of the dead. Warriors who died in battle and women who died in childbirth went to join the Sun god in the sky.

DOLL COMPANION
Colourful figures found in Chancay tombs, such as this one, are called "dolls" because it is believed that they were used in daily life. They were placed with the deceased to serve them in the afterlife.

Mayan child's burial urn

MUMMY OF DEAD KING
In Andean society, mummies were looked after as if they were alive. The living often consulted the dead about important matters. At special festivals, the mummies of emperors were paraded in the streets.

ALL WRAPPED UP
Many mummy bundles have been discovered in the Andean region. The corpse was placed in a flexed position and bound with cord to help maintain the pose. It was then wrapped in textiles and seated upright. Goods were placed around the mummy in the grave.

THE RICH AND THE POOR
The more goods that were placed in a grave, the better off the individual was. Wooden figurines, such as this one of a man, have been found in many Andean tombs. But tombs filled with golden objects, and where the corpse has been more elaborately prepared, indicate that everyone was not equal.

MAYAN BURIAL
The Maya usually buried their dead under house floors or in the ground. Sometimes, however, they cremated the remains or buried them in caves, underground tanks, or urns. The privileged classes were buried in very elaborate tombs. One common type of burial for children was to place the corpse in a large urn, which was then covered by a tripod (three-legged) vessel or pot fragment.

VOLCANO BOY
In 1999, the mummies of two girls and a boy were found on top of Mount Llullaillaco, a volcano in Argentina. Their bodies had been so well preserved by the cold that their internal organs were still intact.

Mummy of a seven-year-old boy found on Mount Llullaillaco, Argentina

Mummy wrapped in reed matting

MIXTEC MUMMY BUNDLE
Mesoamerican mummies were wrapped in a similar way to those from South America. A mask was attached to the face of the mummy. The mask was usually made of stone, but some mummies wore wooden masks. People thought their masks would protect the deceased from the dangers of the afterlife.

Stone mask

RITES OF DEATH
This illustration from the Codex Magliabechiano depicts the burial ritual of a high-ranking Aztec. The dead man is mourned by his family, who make offerings before his mummy bundle and give him *cacauatl* (chocolate) for his journey to the next world.

MUMMY CLOTH
Due to the dry climate of Peru's northern coastal region, all the materials and objects buried with mummies in this area have been beautifully preserved. This woollen mummy cloth bearing the figure of a god with arms outstretched is a typical Peruvian mummy adornment.

Mummy bundle tied up with ropes

Pot found with mummy in grave

Human sacrifice

SACRIFICE WAS A RELIGIOUS RITUAL in Mesoamerica and in the Inca region of South America. The Incas and the Aztecs held special ceremonies that involved sacrifice in temples or on mountain tops, while the Maya sometimes sacrificed victims in wells. Priests performed the sacrifices, which mainly took place at important festivals throughout the year. Sacrifices were also made in times of crisis and to mark special events. The victims included men, women, and children – and sometimes animals. It was common for the Incas to ritually strangle women, while the Maya sometimes drowned their victims and the Aztecs removed the victim's heart. Most sacrifices were performed in honour of the Sun, rain, and earth gods. Human sacrifice was an act of communion with the gods: it was considered necessary to feed the gods to maintain the cosmic order. People believed that as the gods had sacrificed themselves during the creation of the Sun and the Moon, they had to do the same.

SACRIFICIAL KNIFE
This decorated flint knife was found in the Great Temple of the Aztecs (pp.30–31). Stone knives like this were used to kill sacrificial victims.

Eyes made of shell and pyrite

Skull mask found among the offerings in the Great Temple, Tenochtitlan

Sacrificial knives were probably inserted in the nose and mouth to intimidate enemies

SACRIFICE
The most common form of sacrifice among the Aztecs was to stretch the victim over a sacrificial stone. Five priests took part – four of them held the limbs, while one took out the heart.

SKULL MASK
This human skull was probably used as a mask in ritual performances. It may have been the skull of a sacrificial victim.

AFTER SACRIFICE

Once an Aztec priest had taken the heart out, it was placed in a receptacle like the one below. The victim was then thrown down the temple stairs. The body was picked up and part of it, such as the thigh, was given as a reward to the victim's captor. The Aztecs practised cannibalism in some religious ceremonies under strict regulations. For example, enemy captives were ritually eaten, but only legs or arms could be consumed.

Illustration from Codex Magliabecchiano

The skull symbol often appears in Aztec art

SACRIFICIAL STONES AND VESSELS

This ritual vessel (right) may have been intended to contain the blood or the hearts of sacrificial victims. The outer surface is decorated with skulls. The skull was a symbol of fame, glory, or defeat, depending on the situation. The stone below is one kind of stone that was used for the act of sacrifice. The victim would have been stretched over this stone while having his or her heart plucked out.

Ritual vessel

Sacrificial stone

PRECIOUS HEART

This beautifully carved greenstone heart represents the most precious organ that the Aztecs could offer to their gods. Likewise, jade was considered the most valuable stone and the most precious material, far more so than gold. Jade was the symbol of life and agriculture.

MOUNTAIN-TOP SACRIFICE

The tops of high mountains and volcanoes were sacred places. Here people worshipped the earth gods, who were the providers of water and agriculture, and made human sacrifices to them. Water was considered to be the blood of agricultural life. Human sacrifices were performed for many reasons. They were generally considered a present to the gods in exchange for a favour requested such as a good harvest. Those who were sacrificed were thought to be fortunate, since they were guaranteed a life of ease in the world to come.

Ornate Moche water pot depicting men sitting high up in the mountain peaks

FLAYED ALIVE

This 19th-century illustration shows human sacrifice by flaying, or skinning a man alive. The ancient Peruvians performed this kind of ritual sacrifice. Skinning was also practised by the ancient Mexicans during agricultural festivities. Like the ancient Mexicans, the ancient Peruvians had many sacrificial victims dedicated to the Sun, Inti, or to the creator god, Viracocha.

Medicine

IN MESOAMERICA and in the Andean cultures, treatments for illnesses were a mixture of magic and knowledge of the body. Mesoamerican midwives, healers, and physicians were often women who were well versed in the use of herbs. The Andeans believed that disease had a supernatural cause. They treated the sick with herbs for both magical and medicinal reasons. The Aztecs used certain minerals for medicine, as well as the flesh of some animals. The Incas used urine for treating fever, and often bled themselves. Inca surgeons bored holes in the skull and amputated limbs when necessary. Both Mesoamericans and Andeans used obsidian knives and lancets for surgery.

Drinking a herbal infusion to treat fever

Snakeroot, taken for stomach pains

Pudding pipe-tree, a laxative, taken for coughs and fever

MEDICINE SELECTION
Various plants and herbs were used as medicine. The rabbit fern root was taken as a remedy for rheumatism and to treat bites by poisonous animals. Some roots were particularly useful for treating kidney complaints, and palm nuts were taken for circulation ailments. Despite its bitter taste, quinine (from the bark of a Peruvian tree) was taken to prevent and treat malaria.

Rabbit fern, taken for rheumatism

Palm nuts, taken for circulation problems

Quinine, taken for malaria

BANDAGING A LEG
Physicians had a good knowledge of the body, and they were often right in their diagnoses. This Aztec surgeon is bandaging an injured leg.

MAN SUFFERING FROM TUBERCULOSIS
Like the Andeans, the Aztecs also portrayed diseases and deformities in their art. This sculpture is of a man suffering from tuberculosis, one of the most serious ailments in ancient Mexico. Tuberculosis afflicted many young people. The realism of the sculpture allows us to see the deformed back caused by the disease.

POTTERY MAN WITH SPOTS
Although the Spanish *conquistadores* brought many unknown diseases into South America, the Andeans seem to have known some serious diseases before their arrival, including *uta* (a type of leprosy) and syphilis. The man portrayed on this Chancay vessel may have suffered from either disease.

Peyote cactus

Peyote has long roots

MARKET MEDICINE STALL

In Mesoamerica, wild plants and herbs were cultivated in botanical gardens for medicinal purposes and sold in markets. There were roots, seeds, magucy leaves, *copal* resin, and many other types of plant for treating a range of ailments, from snake bites to gout and fever. The ancient Mexicans believed that *copal* smoke cured diseases. Tobacco powder was inhaled by the Andeans to help clear the head, but in Mesoamerica it was also smoked for pleasure. Many seeds and roots were combined with vanilla, cocoa, and maize to make the medicine more palatable, although many of these flavourings were considered medicinal in their own right.

CACTUS TOPS

Some plants and seeds, such as *ololiuhqui* (Morning glory) seeds, were taken by the ancient Mexicans as medicines. Along with the tops of the peyote cactus (above) from northern Mexico, these seeds were also widely taken as drugs. People who ate them experienced colourful hallucinations. Drugs that caused hallucinations were also consumed in order for people to communicate with the gods.

Snakeskins and snake flesh were taken for various illnesses

Nuts and seeds

Leaves and roots

Writing and counting

BOTH THE MESOAMERICAN PEOPLE and the ancient Peruvians kept records. However, what they recorded and how they did this was very different. Mesoamerican cultures had a picture-writing system and kept details of their history and administration, while the Peruvians had no written records. The Incas recorded information about tribute (p.27) and goods in storage on an arrangement of knotted strings called a *quipu*. Many Mesoamerican pictures (or glyphs) were pictograms, in which an object or an idea was represented by a drawing – for example, a shield and a club signified war. This type of writing was kept in books called codices, painted on walls and vases, and carved into a variety of objects, from stone monuments to tiny pieces of jade. The Mesoamericans were obsessed by counting and the passage of time. Both the Aztecs and the Maya devised a vegisimal counting system (based on units of 20), and they had two calendars – the solar calendar and the sacred almanac.

ANCIENT AZTEC GODS
According to Aztec mythology, the most ancient gods and the creators of the universe were "Lord and Lady of our Austenance". They are associated with time and the calendar.

Knotted strings hang from horizontal cord

HIGH SOCIETY
Only the elite, a small fraction of Mesoamerican society, could read and interpret written records. This Mayan woman is reading a book on her knee.

AZTEC DAYS OF THE MONTH
The Aztec solar calendar year was 365 days long. It consisted of 18 months of 20 days and five extra days that were thought to be unlucky. This illustration shows four days of the month – flint knife, rain, flower, and alligator.

MAYAN PAINTED BOOK
Codices were made of paper, cloth made from fibres of the maguey plant, or animal skin. There are four Mayan codices in existence. This one, the Codex Tro-Cortesianus, contains information about divination (predicting the future) and rituals for Mayan priests. Mayan codices were written or painted with fine brushes onto long strips of bark paper that were covered with a layer of chalky paste (gesso) and folded like screens.

Numbers recorded with knots of varying sizes

Facsimile copy of original Codex Tro-Cortesianus

INCA COUNTING DEVICE
The *quipu* was a length of cord held horizontally, from which hung knotted strings of various thicknesses and colours. The information recorded varied according to the types of knots, the cord's length, and the colour and position of the strings. The *quipu* was probably used to record the census and for taxation purposes.

INCA ACCOUNTANT
A special accountant was in charge of keeping records. He was skilled in recording figures, whether of people, llamas, or what tribute was to be paid.

Sun, or Lord of the Earth

AZTEC SUN STONE

This stone is one of the largest Aztec sculptures ever found, measuring about 4 m (13 ft) in diameter. At the centre of the stone is the face of the Sun, or that of the Lord of the Earth. This carving is sometimes called the Calendar Stone, but it actually represents the Aztec belief that the Universe had already passed through four world creations, which had all been destroyed. We are now in the fifth creation, which is doomed to be destroyed by earthquakes. According to Aztec mythology, the Sun, the Moon, and human beings were successfully created at the beginning of the fifth era.

One of the previous four world creations

This band shows the 20 days of the month

The date glyph on this sculpture is "day one death"

RIDDLE OF THE GLYPHS

The study of Mayan hieroglyphic writing began in 1827. By 1950, names of gods and animals had been identified. In 1960, researchers realized that Mayan inscriptions were primarily historical. They deal with the births, accessions, wars, deaths, and marriages of Mayan kings. This Mayan stone carving was placed over doors and windows. It has a glyph that dates it to the 6th century CE.

BUNDLE OF YEARS

The Aztecs divided time into "centuries" of 52 years. At the end of each cycle and the beginning of a new one, an Aztec ceremony called "the binding of the years" took place. In sculpture, each cycle is represented by a bundle of reeds accompanied by dates. This sculpted stone bundle symbolizes the death of an Aztec century.

Bars and dots are Mayan glyphs for numbers

Codex was read from top to bottom, and from left to right

Glyphs showing five gods

Fine layer of gesso (chalky paste)

Weaving and spinning

Nazca textile with fringed border

NO OTHER PEOPLE in the Americas left such a wealth of marvellous woven textiles as the ancient Peruvians. Their exquisitely worked textiles have survived in graves in desert-like areas of Peru. The tradition of weaving and spinning was practised by all women, both in Mesoamerica and in the Andean region. They were expected to spin and weave for their families' needs, and also provide woven goods for payment of tribute and taxes to their rulers. Textiles were woven mainly from cotton and maguey fibre in Mesoamerica, while alpaca and llama wool were widely used in the Andean region.

Andean woman weaving on a back-strap loom

NATURAL DYES
In Mesoamerica, cotton was used for making textiles for the upper classes; maguey, yucca, and other fibres were woven for the commoners. The yarn was dyed before it was woven. Some dyes were made from the juice of flowers and fruits, but dyes were also extracted from shellfish and from the cochineal – a tiny insect that lives on the cactus plant.

BACK-STRAP LOOM
The most common loom used in the Americas was the back-strap loom. It is still widely used today. The loom consists of two loom bars, which are poles that hold the warp (vertical) threads. One bar is hooked to a support such as a tree or post, while the other is secured by a belt around the weaver's back. When the warp is stretched taut, the weft (horizontal) thread is passed under and over the strands of the warp using a heddle stick and a shed rod to lift up alternate strands. To alter the pattern or introduce more colour, more heddles are used, or different groups of warp threads are lifted up.

Loom bar, attached to a tree or post

Long threads fixed to the loom bars are called the warp

Shed rod

Heddle stick grasped with left hand

Weft threads run alternately under and over warp threads

Weaving sword used to smooth down weft threads

Back-strap loom

Strap fitted around weaver's waist

Figurine may be of Mayan goddess Ixchel, patroness of weaving

MAYAN LADY WEAVING
This Mayan figurine shows a young lady sitting on the ground, weaving with a back-strap loom.

DECORATED BORDER
The majority of ancient Peruvian textiles were decorated with motifs, which varied from abstract geometric shapes – squares, oblongs, and frets – to stylized images of birds, fish, animals, and human beings.

Inca woman spinning and twisting as she walks

FABRIC QUALITY
The quality of woven fabrics depended on the quality of the yarn and how finely it was spun.

EMBROIDERED TEXTILE
The ancient Peruvians were rich skilled embroiderers. They created fantastic images with just a few stitches. This Inca woven textile has an embroidered design of stylized heads and serpents, perhaps symbolizing thunder.

Bamboo needle case

NEEDLECASE
Needles were useful weaving tools and were kept safely in cases like this bamboo example. Used for sewing and darning as well as for weaving, needles were made of cactus spines or copper.

Needles made of cactus spines

Wooden whorl

Decorated weaving tool found in work-basket

NAZCA WEAVER
The Nazca culture was renowned for its beautiful textiles. They decorated their pottery with designs that they also used in their weavings. This pot shows a person holding a spindle in one hand.

Spindle and whorl

HOW TO SPIN
With the spindle upright, the spindle and whorl are spun between the fingers. This teases out the yarn, which is then twisted into a fine thread and wound around the spindle.

Ball of unspun cotton

Spindle with spun cotton yarn wound around it

REED WORK-BASKET
This Peruvian reed work-basket contains balls of yarn, spindles, and raw cotton. Reed work-baskets were often buried with their owners so that women could continue weaving in the afterlife. Most weaving probably took place in the outer courtyards of dwellings. Women and men were required to weave, spin, and produce cloth and cord for the empire as a form of taxation. The weaving was done by women, while men made the cloth and cord.

Dyed cotton thread

Women kept their sewing and weaving tools in baskets like this one

Clothes and accessories

CLOTHING STYLES WERE VERY DIFFERENT in Mesoamerica and South America, but in both regions they reflected a person's social class. People who wore clothes made of fine material with colourful and elaborate decoration were of high status. The Incas made their clothes mainly from wool, although on the coast cotton was preferred. Ordinary people wore alpaca-wool garments; silky vicuña wool was worn by the nobles. Mesoamerican clothes were made from cotton or other plant fibres. All items of clothing were very simple. Many were just a piece of material draped around a part of the body. Men from both regions wore loincloths. Aztec women wore a skirt wrapped around the hips, and men wore cloaks draped over the shoulder. Ponchos and tunics slipped over the head and were sewn at the sides.

CAPPING IT ALL
In the Andean region, people wore knitted wool or cotton caps. This handsome Chimu woollen cap with colourful panels is unusual, being woven, not knitted.

SANDAL
The Incas made sandals with leather from the neck of the llama. In other regions, sandals were made of wool or, as in this case, the fibre of the aloe plant.

Plaited wool fastening

IN THE BAG
All Peruvian men carried a small bag under their cloak, slung over the shoulder. In it they carried *coca* leaves for chewing and amulets (good-luck charms).

SLEEVELESS PONCHO *right*
Some ponchos were decorated with fine patterns. They were such important garments that the dead were buried with ponchos. In the highland regions of Peru, both men and women still wear ponchos today.

Woven headband

ANDEAN WOMAN'S DRESS
Although this is an 18th-century impression of a Peruvian woman, her clothing is similar to that worn by an Inca woman: a long dress of woven rectangular cloth, with a long cloak and sandals.

CHILD'S PONCHO *left*
Finely woven ponchos have been discovered covering mummies in some ancient Peruvian graves. This small poncho was found in a child's grave. It is woven from wool, with a design of birds in diagonal bands.

SHELL NECKLACE
In Mesoamerica, only the ruler and nobles could wear jewellery such as headbands, armbands, or nose, lip, and ear plugs. Even necklaces made of shells, like this one, could not be worn by everyone.

DIFFERENT CLOTHES, DIFFERENT JOBS
Aztec people wore clothes that suited their role in society. The lavish headdresses and rich materials worn here show that these are people of high rank.

COORDINATED CLOTHES
This Mayan woman is wearing a matching turban, skirt, and shawl. Her beautiful long hair is tied back with white ribbons. She wears a feather ornament in one ear and a bracelet that is probably made of leather.

Parasol

Elaborate headdress with two folds

SOPHISTICATED LADY
This richly attired figure is obviously a high-ranking Mayan woman. She wears a headdress with two folds, and blue ear plugs that perhaps represent turquoise. Her beaded necklace is similar in shape to Mayan jade necklaces, and she wears bracelets on both arms. With one hand she protects her face with a parasol.

FANCY CAPE
Capes like this one were worn throughout Mesoamerica. This army commander is of a high rank, so his cape is finely decorated.

Robe with holes for arms and square-cut neck

MALE FASHION
This life-sized head of a Mixtec man shows what adornments they wore. He has a headband tied around his forehead, with a bird's head at the centre and blue discs at the sides. His hair is loose, and he wears round blue ear plugs. His mouth is painted with black and white spots, resembling a mouth ornament.

Mayan women often walked barefoot

Master potters

MAYAN FRESCO VASE
The cylindrical pot, such as this one decorated with a jaguar figure, was a common form of Mayan pottery. It was covered with stucco (plaster) and painted over while still wet.

THE DECORATED CERAMICS of ancient Andean cultures are one of their most striking achievements. The Mesoamericans also had a rich and varied pottery tradition. Potters did not use a potter's wheel in either region. They produced a wide range of shapes, which they painted, carved, or stamped for decoration. The finest ceramics were for the rich or for ritual use. Pottery for everyday use was more simple. Because the Andean cultures had no writing system, pottery is a valuable source of information about the societies who made it, their religious ideas, and cultural influences.

ARYBALLUS JAR
Inca pottery was of excellent quality and was made in a few standard shapes. The most typical was the aryballus jar, with a conical base and a tall, flaring neck.

Jar used for storing water or possibly chicha beer

STIRRUP-SPOUTED MOCHE FROG VESSEL
Moche potters based their designs on both fanciful and realistic images. They modelled many animals, human figures, and plants. Vessels with stirrup spouts often served as libation vessels – containers for making liquid offerings to the gods.

NAZCA POT
The Nazca civilization was distinctive for its pottery, decorated in many colours with both realistic and mythological creatures, such as this being with a human body.

Nazca vessel unrolled to show decoration

Stirrup-spout vessel in the shape of a frog

Jade and shell eyes

Pieces of shell

CHICKEN VESSEL
This is a good example of the creativity and imagination of the potters from Teotihuacan. How a pot was made, its shape, and the motifs decorating it help researchers discover when it was made.

Conch shells adorn body

PAINTING PALETTE
The potters of Teotihuacan used both vegetable and mineral pigments, and it is likely that they used some kind of palette to mix their colours. This pottery object may have been used as a such a palette.

FIGURINE AND MOULD
Made using a mould, this small clay artefact depicts a female figure holding two children. It may represent a midwife or a goddess of fertility and childbirth.

Clay goddess

Mould for goddess

Centre of bowl is decorated with a glyph of a deer

CHOLULA BOWL
The city of Cholula was sacred to the Aztecs, and its pottery was highly prized. One style of decoration used only two colours, as seen on this bowl.

Hummingbird perched on rim

MIXTEC CUP
This beautiful Mixtec cup is decorated with a hummingbird perched on the rim. The base has the characteristic step-fret motif often used by Mixtec artists.

Step-fret motif

This urn contained human ashes

Urn found at the Great Temple of the Aztecs

FUNERARY URN
Some pottery vessels were not painted, but instead the decoration was cut into the surface. The picture on one side of this urn is of a bearded god wearing a necklace. He holds a spear thrower in one hand, and spears in the other.

Featherwork

THE BRIGHT COLOURS and natural sheen of tropical bird feathers made them a valuable item for trade and tribute in Mesoamerica and in the Andean region of South America. Tropical birds were hunted and raised in captivity for their feathers, which were worked into stunning patterns and designs. For the Mesoamericans, the iridescent green feathers of the quetzal were the most prized. The Incas used feathers as part of their dress and wove them into clothing for special occasions. They also used them to decorate headdresses and tunics, and to make mosaics (designs of feathers glued to a backing to decorate hard items such as shields). The skilled Aztec featherworkers made beautiful garments only for the nobility, while the Maya made superb headdresses that were extended at the back to make the wearer look like a bird that had just landed.

FEATHER MOSAICS
Ancient Mexico had a guild of expert featherworkers who used intricate methods of gluing and weaving feather mosaics. These methods were studied and illustrated by a Spanish friar (priest) called Bernardino de Sahagún.

FEATHER SHIRT AND HEADDRESS
This type of feather shirt is known as a poncho. Each of the feathers has been carefully stitched to a cotton cloth to make up the design of stylized owls and fish. Several Peruvian cultures, including the Chimu and the Inca, had expert featherworkers.

Tall feather headdress

Fan made of macaw feathers

Holder formed from plaited brown wool

WAVE OF COLOUR
The ancient Peruvians made very colourful fans using feathers from tropical birds. These fans were useful for keeping cool in hot climates. The Peruvians made many practical objects with feathers – especially the feathers of parrots and macaws, which were their favourite birds.

FEATHER HEADDRESS
This simple Peruvian headdress was possibly made from feathers taken from birds in the Amazon region. Items made from the feathers of exotic birds were status symbols.

Strings were used to tie the headdress around the head

MOCTEZUMA'S HEADDRESS?
This is a replica of a headdress said to have belonged to Moctezuma II, the last Aztec ruler. The headdress may have been part of the booty sent by Cortés to Spain (pp.62–63). It is has green quetzal feathers, blue cotinga feathers, and gold discs.

Headdress contains the feathers of at least 250 birds

Fan has a butterfly on this side and a flower on the other

MEXICAN FAN
This fan was made with the feathers of several species of bird. Sumptuous fans like this were used by dignitaries.

Bamboo handle

Feather heuddress

FEATHERS IN STONE
This carved stone Atlantean figure from a temple at Chichen Itza is dressed in a full-length feather cloak and a feather headdress. It was once painted all over, and the two watercolours show how it would probably have looked.

Cloak of yellow and green feathers

Rear view

Front view

Side view

WARRIOR OUTFIT
An Aztec warrior's rank was reflected in the type of feather suit he wore. This elaborate suit, complete with shield and headdress, was worn by a high-ranking warrior.

Feather headdress

Feather suit belonging to a warrior of high status

Feather shield

REBUILDING THE PAST
Watercolours like the one above by the British artist Adela Breton give us an idea of how sculptures were painted in pre-Hispanic times, and of the original appearance of the buildings at Chichen Itza.

Feather suit

Precious metals

LIP ORNAMENT
Eagle heads like
this one made
by the Mixtecs
were popular as decoration for lip
plugs, or labrets. The Mixtecs produced
most of the gold work for the Aztec
elite. Labrets were inserted through
a hole made below the bottom lip.

THE PERUVIAN TRADITION of crafting
magnificent artefacts from precious metals
began 3,500 years ago, the age of the oldest
piece of precious metalwork found in the
Andes. Methods of metalworking gradually
developed, and metals were widely worked in
South America before the Christian era. They
were introduced to Mesoamerica in about
850 BCE. Some of the most common precious
metals in the Americas are gold, silver, and
platinum. These were mostly used for
making ritual objects, trinkets, and
jewellery. Combinations of gold
and silver, and copper and gold (called *tumbaga*)
were also used. Because of the value attached
to gold, wearing gold jewellery was a sign of
a person's wealth and power. When a wealthy
person died, his or her tomb would be filled
with precious gold and silver objects,
encrusted with precious stones.

GOLD CREATURE
The ancient South
American goldsmiths
produced many fantastic
creatures. This figure is
a mixture of human
and animal forms.

PORTRAIT BEAKER
This type of beaker
is called a portrait
beaker, as it seems
to portray the face
of a real person.
Portrait beakers
were often made
of beaten silver.

*Almond-shaped
eyes*

*Aquiline
nose*

*Beaker has
hammered
bird design*

SILVER BEAKER
These beakers are usually
known as *keros*. Many of
them have been found
throughout the Andean
region, placed in cemeteries
together with other objects
near the corpses. Some *keros*
were used to drink *chicha*, a
kind of beer made of maize.
Some beakers were inlaid with
turquoise. This beaker is the
work of a Chimu metalsmith,
indicating that it was made
before the Inca period.

ELEGANT NECKLACE
Of the few gold objects that have survived from the Basin of Mexico, most have been found at the Great Temple of the Aztecs. The beads of this necklace were made of hollow gold. Some of them are plain, while others are decorated with a spiral design.

BAT RATTLE
This cast-gold rattle represents a bat god. The god is holding a thunderbolt in one hand and a throwing stick in the other.

Thunderbolt

Charcoal-heated furnace, kept hot by blowing through a tube

GOLD IN THE NOSE
This Mixtec ornament is one of the few surviving nose plugs. Some nose ornaments are in the shape of butterflies and other creatures. The beauty of this one lies in its simplicity.

PANNING FOR GOLD
Most of the gold used by the Peruvian Indians was obtained from "placer" mines in rivers, where the gold is near the surface. They used fire-hardened digging sticks to break up the earth, and shallow trays in which to carry and wash it.

Handle has figure of a hummingbird

LIME SCOOPS
These tiny lime scoops were used in the preparation of a drug called *coca*. Powdered lime was scooped onto a *coca* leaf, made into a ball, and chewed.

Figure holds a standard or banner

Hooked earrings

GOLDSMITH
The goldsmith had a high status in Aztec society. He made the most intricate objects using the "lost wax" method. First he made an intricately carved beeswax mould and covered it with a layer of clay. When the mould was heated, the melted wax flowed out, and the mould was filled with molten metal. In this illustration, the goldsmith is about to pour molten gold into a mould.

Handle has figure of a monkey

Stylized Inca llama figure, made of gold

MIXTEC GOLD FIGURE
This figure is probably the work of a Mixtec goldsmith. It shows man holding a shield and darts, with a pendant around his neck from which three bells hang. He is well attired, indicating that he is a member of the elite, a ruler, or an important warrior, and he is clad with gold – in other words, with wealth and power.

GOLD LLAMA
The Incas made vessels and figures using the casting method, by pouring molten metal into a mould. Items like this llama figure were sometimes partly soldered together too.

Precious stones

TURQUOISE NECKLACE
In the Andean region, turquoise was used for making jewellery and for decorating objects such as pots and statues. This necklace was probably made by the Incas.

Necklace made of thick turquoise discs

Red shell beads

THE INCAS, MAYA, AND AZTECS had a taste for all kinds of stones, and their skilled craftsmen fashioned exquisite objects from them. The Mesoamerican people favoured stones of different colours with shiny surfaces, including jade and green stones in general, turquoise, onyx, rock crystal, and porphyry (a dark red rock). They used them to make jewellery and a variety of containers, sculptures, and masks. Jade was the most precious material to the Mesoamerican people. It was associated with water, the life-giving fluid, and with the colour of the maize plant, their staple food. Turquoise was also highly valued and was laboriously worked both in Mesoamerica and in the Andean regions. The Incas used it as inlay in gold and silver objects.

TURQUOISE AND GOLD NECKLACE
Turquoise was highly valued in the Andean region. Only a few artefacts, like this delicate Inca necklace, have survived.

CHIMU WOMAN
This Chimu figurine (left) is of a woman wearing a headdress and a necklace strung with various beads, perhaps shells and stones.

Pieces of turquoise

Hollow gold bead

LIKE FATHER, LIKE SON
Craftsmen, such as this precious-stone cutter (called a lapidary), passed their skills on to their sons, who would take up their trade on reaching manhood. The Aztecs believed that the arts of the lapidary and the goldsmith came from the Toltecs, who had received their skills from the god Quetzalcoatl.

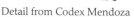

Detail from Codex Mendoza

VAMPIRE BAT
This Zapotec mosaic mask is made of 25 pieces of jade. It is in the shape of a human head covered by a bat mask. The bat was an important symbol in the art of the Zapotec people.

Eyes made of shell

ONYX CUP
In Mesoamerica, onyx was used for making objects for the elite. The craftsman would begin with a large lump of onyx, cutting out the centre with obsidian tools (above). Many onyx objects are rounded, like the cup shown below, as this was the easiest shape to produce.

Eyes and teeth made of shell

TURQUOISE MASK
One of the most remarkable Mesoamerican arts was that of mosaic making, especially using turquoise. This mask, representing the god Quetzalcoatl, is one of the best preserved examples of Mexican turquoise mosaic.

This piece rested behind the lip, against the gum

JADE LABRET
The Mesoamerican labret (lip plug) was an ornament that was worn below the lower lip. The Aztec elite wore labrets made from many different materials, but especially gold and jade.

JADE NECKLACE
This Olmec necklace with a human head was worn by a member of the elite. The wealthy in Mesoamerica wore many body adornments, such as necklaces and bracelets.

Jade and other green stones were highly valued in Mesoamerica

MASK OF A KING
When the Mayan Lord Pacal died, he was buried below a magnificent temple pyramid at Palenque. His corpse was covered with jewels and objects made from precious stones, such as jade. This jade mosaic mask, with eyes of inlaid shell and obsidian, covered his face. Each of his fingers was adorned with jade rings.

Coyote with jaws wide open

Mother-of-pearl

Warrior's face peering out of coyote mask

COYOTE WARRIOR
This Toltec ornament is a unique example of Toltec craftsmanship. It is also unique for what it represents – a coyote warrior from the Toltec city of Tula. The head is covered with mother-of-pearl mosaic.

FANCY TATTOOS
As well as wearing jewellery, Mesoamericans tattooed their bodies. This was a widespread practice in the whole of Mesoamerica.

Masks

FOR HUNDREDS OF YEARS, masks fashioned from materials such as gold, obsidian, jade, and wood – some inlaid with turquoise and coral – have been worn in the Americas. Masks were commonly placed over mummy bundles to protect the deceased from the dangers of the afterlife. They were also worn during festivals. Among the Incas and the Aztecs, for whom music and dance (pp.56–57) were a form of religious expression, masks and costumes had a symbolic meaning. Even today, people in Mesoamerica and in the Andean region still wear masks for festivals.

HUMAN MASK
Found at the Great Temple of the Aztecs, this finely carved greenstone mask was an offering to the gods. It is inlaid with shell and obsidian, and its ear lobes are pierced so that ear plugs can be attached.

Jade ear plug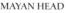

BEATEN COPPER MASK
Masks such as this copper one (left) have been found on mummies in many Andean burial sites. The wealthier the individual, the more elaborate was their burial – and the more expensive the fabrics that wrapped and decorated the mummy bundle.

Mask made of stone

Holes in mask may have had hair threaded through them

FACE VALUE
Many objects from the Mezcala region, including masks, were found at the Great Temple of the Aztecs. This mask was paid as tribute to the Aztecs (pp.26–27).

MAYAN HEAD
Many heads and masks give an idea of what people looked like. This head shows that the Maya practised cranial deformation, which means that they forced the top of the head to grow taller and slope backwards.

JEWELLED MASK
This Chimu funerary mask is made of thin sheet-gold. It would have been placed over a mummy's face. The nose ornament, decorated with gold discs, was made separately.

Eyes decorated with emerald beads

Eyes made of shell

Real hair attached to mask

MASK FROM ANCON
Masks of all shapes, colours, and sizes have been found in Peruvian burial sites. This one was found covering a mummy's face in an enormous cemetery at Ancon, on the central coast of Peru.

Turquoise mosaic pieces

TEOTIHUACAN MASK
Teotihuacan is famous for its expert mask makers, who made realistic masks from a variety of materials. This mask has mosaic pieces of turquoise and coral around the nose plug. The pupils of the eyes are made of obsidian, while the whites are shell inlays.

Cloth hat with real hair

Necklace made from coral beads

Snarling, cat-like face

REMARKABLE OFFERING
The Chancay tombs of southern Peru contained seated figures dressed in remarkable textiles and wooden masks. Many of these were buried with the deceased as offerings to the gods.

HALF-FELINE, HALF-HUMAN MASK
Olmec art drew its inspiration from mythology and religion. One of the Olmecs' beliefs was that a woman was united with a jaguar, producing a race with both features, as can be seen in this jade mask.

Music and dance

MOCHE FLAUTIST
Many Moche vases are realistic portraits of people and their pastimes. This one shows that flutes were played in the Andean region.

MUSIC, SONG, AND DANCE were an important part of Mesoamerican and South American life. Scenes of people playing music and dancing decorate many pottery vases, especially those produced by the Moche potters. The most common instruments in both Mesoamerica and South America were rattles, whistles, trumpets, flutes, copper bells, and shells. String instruments were practically unknown in the Americas. The music in South America was not very varied, and often musical instruments only played one tone. For these civilizations, music and dance were closely linked to religion. Everyone, from rulers to peasants, took part in dances that were performed especially for their gods.

End of rattle in the shape of a dog's head

CLAY TRUMPET
Moche trumpets came in straight and coiled shapes. The one shown here ends in two cat-like heads, which may represent a god. This shape of coil is typical of Moche trumpets.

Cat-like heads have gaping, snarling jaws with bared fangs

Carving shows a person with loose hair, wearing a tasselled headdress decorated with feathers

Aztec *teponaztli* (horizontal drum)

Pole decorated with paper sheets and flags

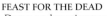

FEAST FOR THE DEAD
Dance and music were an important part of feasts and ritual occasions. This illustration shows men holding hands, dancing around a pole, at a feast for the dead. The pole is festooned with paper sheets and three big flags, one of which has a feather decoration. The Aztecs adorned an image of the dead person with flags. This feast lasted all day, and people danced to the beat of the drum, played by a priest. The dancers in this scene were captives who were later burned as sacrifice.

Drum covered with a cat's pelt

INCA PANPIPES
The most commonly played Andean musical instrument was the syrinx, or panpipes, which were usually made from cane or pottery. Delicate sounds are produced by blowing across one end of the panpipes. These Inca panpipes are made from the quills of a bird of prey called the condor.

Quills held together by a horizontal quill, tied with string

Punpipes are made of tubes of different lengths

POTTERY RATTLE
Rattles were made of pottery, metal, or strings of large seeds. This Moche rattle has a dog's head at one end. The handle of the rattle is in the shape of a man's head.

Man's head

MUSICAL CELEBRATIONS
Most Inca instruments were wind and percussion instruments. In this fiesta scene, the women are singing, dancing, and playing the drum, while the men are playing flutes, or *quenas*.

BEATING THE RHYTHM *below*
In Aztec times, two types of drum were played, called the *teponaztli* (horizontal drum) and the *huehuetl* or *tlapanhuehuetl* (vertical drum). The *teponaztli*, shown below, was a hollowed-out log with a hole in the bottom and slotted at the top. It was played using drumsticks with rubber tips. The codex illustration at right shows an Aztec orchestra with a similar drum. The decoration of drums varied from intricate carvings to realistic animal or human forms. Some drums had carvings that alluded to warfare. Drums were played before setting off to war.

AZTEC ORCHESTRA
Gourd (or gourd-shaped) rattles were an essential part of music. They are depicted in Aztec books and in Mayan mural paintings. This illustration shows men shaking rattles and two drummers, one playing the *huehuetl* (centre left) and the other the *teponaztli* (centre right).

UNIQUE FLUTE
The Mesoamerican people played a wide range of flutes, from simple, straight ones to more complex ones such as this, decorated with a figure of a woman, standing on a disc that has several openings. This type of flute is unique to Mesoamerica. It was probably played in religious ceremonies.

Sports and games

EVERY ASPECT of Aztec life revolved around religion, including sports and games. The two main games played by the Aztecs were *patolli*, a board game similar to backgammon, and the ball-game *ulama*, which was played in Mesoamerica long before the Aztecs by other ancient Mexican civilizations such as the Maya. As well as being a sport, the ball-game had a religious meaning. The ball-court represented the world and the ball stood for the Moon and the Sun. Bets were placed on the outcome of the game, and some players lost everything they had – including their lives.

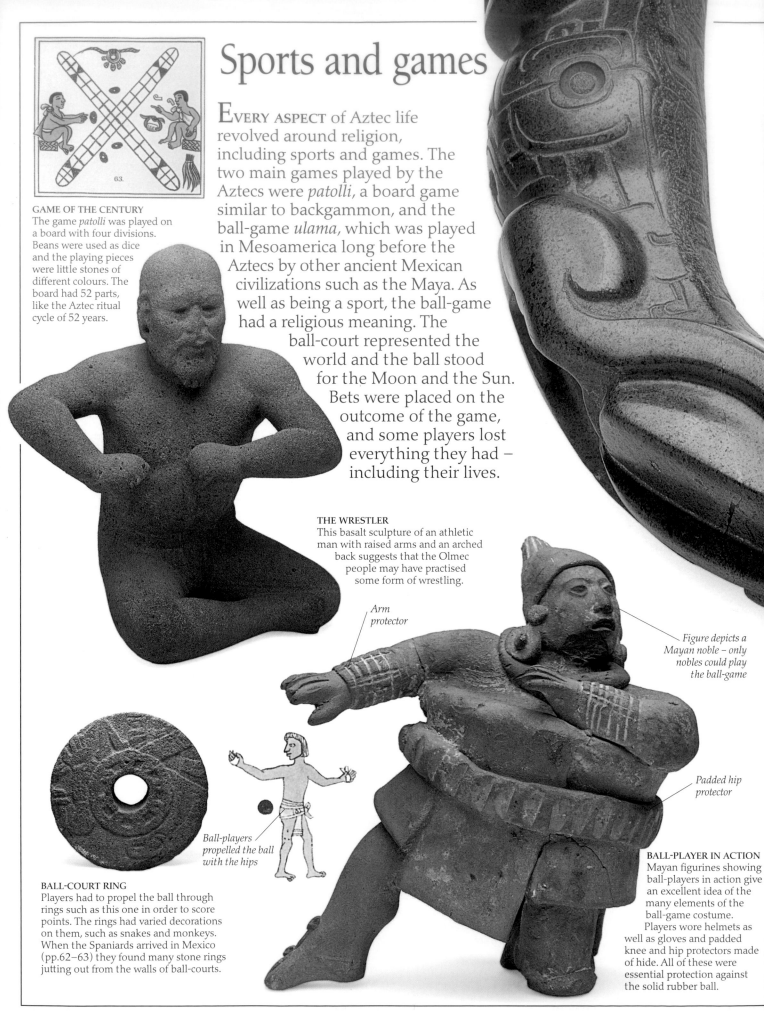

GAME OF THE CENTURY
The game *patolli* was played on a board with four divisions. Beans were used as dice and the playing pieces were little stones of different colours. The board had 52 parts, like the Aztec ritual cycle of 52 years.

THE WRESTLER
This basalt sculpture of an athletic man with raised arms and an arched back suggests that the Olmec people may have practised some form of wrestling.

Arm protector

Figure depicts a Mayan noble – only nobles could play the ball-game

Padded hip protector

Ball-players propelled the ball with the hips

BALL-COURT RING
Players had to propel the ball through rings such as this one in order to score points. The rings had varied decorations on them, such as snakes and monkeys. When the Spaniards arrived in Mexico (pp.62–63) they found many stone rings jutting out from the walls of ball-courts.

BALL-PLAYER IN ACTION
Mayan figurines showing ball-players in action give an excellent idea of the many elements of the ball-game costume. Players wore helmets as well as gloves and padded knee and hip protectors made of hide. All of these were essential protection against the solid rubber ball.

58

STONE AXEHEAD
Hachas, or axes, were used by several Mesoamerican cultures as part of the ball-game. *Hachas* may have been worn attached to the front of the yoke in ritual processions.

Axe in the shape of a human head

Elaborately carved greenstone yoke

BALL-COURT
This ball-court at Chichen Itza is shaped like a capital I. To aim the ball through the rings was extremely difficult as the rings were set 8 m (27 ft) high.

PLAYING BALL
Although no-one knows exactly how the ball-game was played, we do know that it was played by two teams, each of two or three players, using a solid rubber ball in specially made courts. It was a dangerous game, because of the speed at which the solid rubber ball was propelled from one side of the court to the other using the hips – using hands and feet was not allowed. The game varied according to when and where it was played.

GREENSTONE YOKE
Yugos, or stone yokes, (left) and axes (above left) such as these beautifully carved ones are probably replicas of wooden or leather paraphernalia used in the ceremonial ball-game. Large, horseshoe-shaped yokes were worn around the waist of the player as protective belts. Stone yokes were probably used as moulds for making copies in leather or wood.

Marker is about 2 m (6.5 ft) tall

MARKER POST
Tall stone markers, such as this one, were placed on each side of the ball-court. In Mayan courts there were as many as three markers set into the ground. It is not clear how the game was scored, or exactly what the markers were used for.

Blood in the form of snakes

SYMBOLIC GAME
There were many beliefs surrounding the ball-game. The game's violent competition was a symbol of the battle between darkness (night) and light (day), and was a re-enactment of the death and rebirth of the Sun. People also believed that the more they played the ball-game, the better their harvest would be.

Ball-court ring

Codex illustration of a ball-court

LOSER LOSES ALL
The stakes were high for the opposing teams in a ball-game. The losing team was often sacrificed. This sculpted panel shows a decapitated ball-player. The blood streaming from his neck is pictured as snakes, which were symbols of agricultural fertility.

Bestiary

ANIMAL LIFE IN MESOMERICA and South America was rich and varied. Animals played an important part in everyday life and also in religion. Many works of art included images of animals that were significant to the local people, such as foxes, owls, jaguars, llamas, hummingbirds, and eagles. Some animals were domesticated – for example, the turkey and the dog in Mesoamerica, and the llama and the alpaca in the Andean region. With their relatives, the guanacos and vicuñas, llamas and alpacas were valued for their wool and meat, and also as beasts of burden. Deer, rabbits, ducks, and many other kinds of edible bird abounded in both regions. The tropical forests were home to the jaguar, the largest cat in the world, which was worshipped and feared along with snakes.

BIRD ASSORTMENT
Mesoamerica had a variety of brilliantly coloured tropical birds, including parrots, macaws, and quetzals. Their feathers were used to decorate a range of objects and clothes (pp.48–49).

QUETZAL BIRD
This bird was greatly valued by the ancient Mesoamericans, for whom its long, deep-green feathers were as precious as jade or gold. Some of their gods were covered in quetzal feathers, and the bird's feathers were also used to make the headdresses of rulers and kings.

This an example of plumbate pottery – lead in the clay gives the pot a metallic finish

BIRD TAPESTRY
The Andean Paracas culture was renowned for its abundant, ornate textiles that were placed alongside the dead. This textile fragment is decorated with a typical Paracas design of stylized birds.

Figure has feline claws and ears and a stylized tail

FABRIC ANIMAL
Many textiles from Paracas are woven or embroidered with animal images, often in a stylized form. Sometimes it is difficult to identify the animal in question, because of the geometric forms.

FOX
Animals that hunted and killed other animals, such as the fox, were in turn hunted by the Aztecs and the Incas. This Moche vessel depicts the face of a snarling fox.

TOLTEC CERAMIC DOG
Some breeds of dog were fattened and eaten by the Aztecs and the Maya, but the Incas considered eating dog meat a disgusting habit. The Mesoamericans used dogs as companions in hunting expeditions. According to their religion, dogs were also necessary for the journey to the afterlife, as they helped the dead cross rivers.

Stirrup-spouted Moche vessel in the form of a fox's head.

Vicuñas on the grasslands of the Andean mountains

ARMADILLO
The Aztecs ate the meat of the armadillo, which is white and tastes like chicken. Among the Maya, the armadillo was associated with the afterlife.

Some armadillos grow to a length of 120 cm (4 ft)

The armadillo is a nocturnal mammal that lives in tropical areas

Alpacas can reach a height of 130 cm (50 in) at the shoulder

ALPACA
The alpaca lives in the Andean highlands. It was kept in herds by the ancient Peruvians because, along with the vicuña, its long wool was ideal for weaving. Its relatives, the guanaco and the llama, were killed for food, although the llama was mostly used for carrying loads. The ancient Andean people made offerings to the alpaca, because it made an important contribution to their livelihood.

VICUÑAS
Like the alpaca, the vicuña (above) was a good wool-producing animal. Vicuñas gave the most elegant, silk-like wool. Garments woven from vicuña wool were worn by the Inca nobility.

Zapotec jaguar vessel, probably used as an incense burner

Ocelot

OCELOT
This wild cat is sometimes known as the Mexican tiger. The ocelot was a greatly feared creature. Some warriors wore ocelot skins when going into battle.

Puma

PUMA
The puma is found in a wide range of habitats in the Americas, including mountains and tropical forests. It was hunted for its skin by ancient American peoples.

Jaguar

SACRED JAGUAR
The jaguar was one of the most powerful symbols in Mesoamerica and South America. Its strength, ferocity, cunning, and hunting ability were greatly admired. The Zapotec vessel (far right) is in the shape of a jaguar standing on three legs.

Leg decorated with head of baby jaguar

The Spanish conquest

WHEN THE SPANISH ARRIVED in the Americas, they knew nothing about the Mesoamerican and Andean cultures with their powerful empires, elaborate palaces, and religions that reached into every part of their life. Neither did the inhabitants of the Americas have any knowledge of the Spanish. Many omens had forewarned Moctezuma II, the Aztec ruler, of an imminent disaster. The Inca ruler Huayna Capac, too, had heard that strange, bearded men had appeared on the coast. Hernándo Cortés entered Mexico in 1519 and Francisco Pizarro arrived in Peru in 1532. Although having few soldiers, the Spanish armies, with their horses and cannons, were stronger. Many local people joined forces with the Spaniards, angry at having to pay heavy tributes. Within a short time, the world of the Aztecs and the Incas was destroyed, their temples razed to the ground, and their emperors murdered. The Maya resisted until 1542, when the Spanish established a capital at Mérida.

MOCTEZUMA GREETS CORTÉS
When they first met, Cortés greeted Moctezuma with a bow, and Moctezuma handed him splendid presents of gold, precious stones such as jade, and feather objects. Cortés was on horseback and Moctezuma was carried in a litter. The Spanish soldiers were dressed in steel armour while the Aztecs wore simple cotton cloaks. This meeting would prove decisive in the conquest of Mexico. Moctezuma at this point was in two minds about the true nature of Cortés – was he human or god, their enemy or their saviour? The events that followed proved Cortés to be the former.

MASSACRE
The Spanish *conquistadores* went in search of riches. If they met any resistance from the native people, the *conquistadores* killed them. This illustration depicts an expedition to Michoacan in the west of Mexico, where many local noblemen were killed for refusing to say where their treasures were hidden.

Warriors from the state of Tlaxcala supported the conquistadores

GOLDEN DEATH
This scene from the Codex Kingsborough shows a Spanish tribute collector punishing the Mexican Indians at Tepetlaoztoc. A Spanish tribute collector was a privileged colonialist known as an *encomendero*. The Indians being burned were late in paying their tribute. The tribute demanded consisted of bundles of maize and gold jewellery.

Doubloon coins made from gold mined in South America

A DISEASE THAT ONLY GOLD COULD CURE

To coerce the people of Mesoamerica and South America to give them their gold, the Spanish often told them that they suffered from a disease that only gold could cure. Cortés and Pizarro both went to the Americas in search of gold, and they found a great deal of it. At the start of the conquest, Cortés sent booty to King Charles V of Spain consisting of gold and silver objects and many other goods. Over the years, huge quantities of gold were shipped to Spain. Today, the ceilings of many Spanish churches are gilded with gold from the Americas.

PUNISHMENT

This illustration shows some of the punishments inflicted by the Spanish on the Inca people. They included beating them and hanging them upside down. The cruelty of many of the *conquistadores* made some Spanish friars devote their life to denouncing the behaviour of their compatriots.

Francisco Pizarro, the conqueror of Peru

GREED FOR GOLD

This caricature shows a greedy Francisco Pizarro contemplating gold from his new Peruvian mine. Pizarro did not understand the civilization that he helped to destroy.

Wooden Inca *kero*, or beaker

CONQUEROR'S BEAKER

This wooden *kero* beaker portrays the conqueror of Peru, Francisco Pizarro. Under Pizarro, Spanish control was established over the Inca empire. The Spanish forced people to abandon their irrigated lands and demanded that they mine more precious metals. Christianity was imposed upon the Incas, but they were slow to accept the new religion and continued in their old practices. The Incas continued with some of their crafts, such as weaving and making wooden *keros* like this one, which may have been made for Pizarro himself.

Did you know?

AMAZING FACTS

The Maya and the Aztecs were excellent beekeepers. They raised stingless bees for honey, which was harvested once a year for medicine and for sweetening food.

Chewing gum may have been an Aztec innovation. The chicozapote tree, one of the most common in Mesoamerica, produces a resin

Chicozapote tree

known as chicle, from which chewing gum is made. The Aztecs chewed on chicle to clean their teeth.

The Mayan people had a zodiac of constellations made up of animals. These included the turtle, the bat, the jaguar, and the turkey. The only animal common to both Mayan and Western zodiac signs is the scorpion.

The Aztecs used a beverage made from live toads steeped in sugar in some of their religious rituals. Toads of the *Bufo* genus secrete toxins from their parotid glands which, when consumed, produce hallucinations. Many Aztec medicines were based on these secretions.

Some Mayan temples featured a complex mosaic of stonework around the entrance door that gave the impression of the jaws of a monster, including stone snouts and fangs. This is because, in Mayan belief, the entrance to the underworld was thought of as the mouth of a monster. By entering a temple decorated in this way, priests believed they were literally stepping into the supernatural world.

Mayan temple entrance resembling jaws

Many Inca kings kept everything they had contact with, so that they could be buried with it. Tombs have been found containing hampers of used clothing, the king's dishes and cutlery, hair and nail clippings – even corn cobs and old bones once gnawed on by the king.

In Mesoamerica, the jaguar (the largest cat of the Americas) was a symbol of royal power. Kings wore the pelt of a jaguar as part of their regalia, and jaguars were offered to the gods in sacrifice.

The Maya believed that slightly crossed eyes were beautiful. They dangled objects in front of their eyes in an attempt to cross them. Foreheads that sloped back were also considered beautiful. To achieve this, the Maya tied boards to babies' foreheads to mould their skulls into the desired shape. This process did not seem to harm the brain.

The Aztec Calendar Stone, carved in the early 16th century, is immense. It measures around 4 m (13 ft) in diameter and weighs 24 tonnes. The Aztec solar year contained 18 months of 20 days each, with 5 extra days. Aztec priests used the calendar to keep track of important festival dates. The face of the stone contains various mythological and astrological figures and signs. The most important figure in the stone is Tonatiuh, the Sun god, located in the centre.

Mayan artists, unlike those of many ancient cultures, often included their names on stone carvings and other works. There are also Mayan ceramics "signed" with the artist's name.

The large number and wide variety of musical instruments found in archaeological sites in Mesoamerica indicate the important place of music and dance in cultural life. There were drums made of wood or clay topped with monkey skins; rattles made of turtle shells; hollow shakers filled with shells, seeds, or dried llama toenails; conch-shell trumpets; and flutes made from animal or human bones.

Clothing was an important status symbol among the Incas. The king had certain fabrics reserved for his use alone. His shirts were of the finest, most delicate cloth, embroidered with gold and silver and decorated with bird feathers. Some royal clothing was made of such difficult-to-produce fibres as bat hair.

Flute

Figures from mythology are shown on the calendar stone

Modern reconstruction of Aztec calendar

QUESTIONS AND ANSWERS

Q Why was the ball-game, or *ulama* as it was known, so important?

A The Mesoamerican peoples were obsessed with *ulama*, not only as a sport played for general recreation, but also as a religious ritual. The ball-game took place between competing teams of players, and may have symbolized the battles between the sky gods and the lords of the underworld, with the ball itself representing the Sun. In some games, the leader of a losing team was decapitated; his skull then formed the core of a new ball. In other games, the winning team's prize was to behead the unfortunate losers.

Disc inlaid in Mayan ball-court floor

Q What was in the water at the Sacred Cenote at Chichen Itza?

A Cenotes (natural wells formed after the roof of an underground river collapses) were important to the Maya. They considered them to be a way of communicating directly with Chac, the rain god, to ask for plentiful rain for the crops. For hundreds of years, people told tales of fabulous gold and jade objects tossed into these wells to appease Chac. An American consul to the region named Edward Thompson used his diplomatic skills to purchase the lands containing the Sacred Cenote at Chichen Itza, Mexico. Between 1904 and 1907, he hired men to dive into the murky waters and used a simple dredge to pull up hundreds of precious objects (and child-sized human bones). Many of them were removed from the country and displayed in the Peabody Museum in Boston, USA. The Mexican authorities fought for decades for the return of the treasures, and they are now on display in the Regional Museum of Merida, Mexico.

Q Where was the City of the Gods, and why was it sacred to the Aztecs?

A The ruins of Teotihuacan lie just north of present-day Mexico City. Founded around 100 BCE, Teotihuacan grew to become the largest city in the Americas, with a population of about 150,000 people. Two huge step-pyramids, the Pyramid of the Sun and the Pyramid of the Moon, dominated its centre. The Teotihuacan culture declined and the city was abandoned around 750 CE. The Aztecs made the city a pilgrimage site, since they believed that it was where the gods had gathered to create the Sun and the Moon.

View of Teotihuacan ruins along the Avenue of the Dead

Q Who rediscovered Machu Picchu, the lost city of the Incas?

A This incredible city was probably constructed by the Incas in the mid to late 15th century, and was inhabited until the Spanish conquest of Peru. Its large palace and temples surrounding a courtyard were not meant to be a "working" city, but a country retreat for the Inca nobility. The American archaeologist Hiram Bingham, in the area to explore old Inca roads, encountered the city in 1911. He wrote a number of books and articles that introduced Machu Picchu to the rest of the world.

Q What is the mystery behind the Nazca lines in Peru?

A The Nazca people created hundreds of pictures in the Peruvian desert of birds, insects, mammals, fish, and plants. These immense "drawings" were made by arranging small stones on the desert flats. They may have been sacred pathways, as some of the lines meet at small shrines where offerings were made.

Nazca bird figure in the deserts of Peru

Q What happened to the Mesoamerican and Andean peoples after the Spanish conquest?

A Many people were captured and killed by the Spanish *conquistadores*; scores of others died from contact with new European diseases. The Spanish also enslaved people, sending them to mine precious metals. It is important to note that the people did not simply disappear. While Aztec, Inca, and Maya are generally used as historical terms, millions of their descendants still live in the region today, and speak related languages.

Record breakers

OLDEST INTACT MAYAN MURAL
In 2002, archaeologist William Saturno uncovered a near-pristine Mayan mural dating from 100 CE, in San Bartolo, Guatemala

LARGEST BALL-COURT IN MESOAMERICA
The court at Chichen Itza measures 168 m (551 ft) long and 70 m (229 ft) wide. Its acoustics are so good that you can stand at one end and hear people talking at the other.

TALLEST MAYAN PYRAMID
Erected around 741 CE, Temple IV at Tikal, Guatemala, rises to a height of 70 m (230 ft).

LARGEST ADOBE STRUCTURE IN SOUTH AMERICA
The base of the Temple of the Sun, near Trujillo, Peru, measures 223 m (730 ft) on each side. Built by the Moche, it was originally 70 m (200 ft) high.

LARGEST PREHISTORIC REPRESENTATION OF A HUMAN FIGURE IN THE WORLD
The geoglyph of the Giant of Atacama, located in Iquique, Chile, is 86 m (282 ft) long.

Timeline

THE SPANISH EXPLORERS who reached the Americas in the 16th century called it the New World, but there was nothing new about it to the civilizations they found there. The cultures of the Aztecs and the Maya of Mesoamerica and the Incas of South America had been thriving for centuries, and numerous other civilizations had risen and fallen during the preceding millennia. The people of these civilizations built spectacular cities, created masterpieces of art, established trading links, created religious traditions, and built vast political empires. This timeline will guide you through the cultural history of Mesoamerica and South America.

Moche owl figure

c.13,000 BCE
Asian hunter-gatherers probably make the first crossings into Alaska and the Yukon in North America over the Bering Strait; by c.11,000 BCE, there are people in Chile.

c.7000 BCE
The first crops are grown in Mexico. Maize is first cultivated there in about 5,000 BCE.

c.3500 BCE
The llama is first used as a pack animal in Peru; it is also used as a food source.

c.3500 BCE
Cotton is grown as a crop in Peruvian villages. Women weave cloth from the cotton; they are often buried with their weaving baskets.

Cotton

2000 BCE–250 CE
The Preclassic Period of Mesoamerican history; the Olmecs dominate.

c.1200 BCE
The rise of the Olmecs on the coast of the Gulf of Mexico. The Olmecs (believed to be the first civilization in North and Central America) thrive for 600 years. They are skilled sculptors and architects, as well as fishermen, farmers, and traders.

c.1000 BCE
The Mayan culture of Mesoamerica is well established by now.

c.600 BCE
The Oaxaca culture begins to overtake the Olmec culture. The Zapotec civilization is established with its capital in Monte Alban.

c.500 BCE
The Paracas culture flourishes in Peru. The people are skilled at embroidery, using more than 100 colours in their elaborate works.

c.200 BCE
The Nazca culture begins in southern Peru; its people are known for painted pottery as well as for creating large and mysterious geoglyphs in the desert.

c.100 CE
The Moche civilization on the Peruvian coast begins. The Moche are excellent potters and the first South Americans to produce clay objects from moulds. The people are also highly skilled weavers and goldsmiths.

250–900
The Classic Period of Mesoamerican history; the Maya dominate.

c.250
The Mayan civilization of Guatemala, Honduras, and eastern Mexico enters the period of its greatest development. The Maya do not have a capital city or single ruler. Instead, each city governs itself.

c.600
The Tiahuanaco empire grows near Lake Titicaca in Bolivia, South America. Its people establish a leading trading centre, the vast city of Tiahuanaco, which becomes home to more than 100,000 people. Their Peruvian neighbours, the Huari, share their religion and art styles, and together the two cultures control the entire Andean region.

c.650
The Pyramid of the Sun is the centre of civilization for the mighty Teotihuacan culture in Mexico. It is part of a large complex, linked by wide, straight streets, that comprises several vast pyramids, palaces, and other buildings of unknown use.

Pyramid of the Sun,
Teotihuacan

c.850
The Mayan civilization in the southern part of Mexico begins to fade. Over the next 200 years, Mayan control of northern Mexico also wanes. Battling empires emerge to take control of the region.

900–1519
The Postclassic Period of history in Mesoamerica.

c.900–1000
The Toltecs build a capital at Tula, Mexico. Their culture blends aspects of Mayan culture with their own. They are excellent architects and artisans, and worship Quetzalcoatl (the Feathered Serpent) as a man-god. The Toltecs eventually settle in Chichen Itza and build amazing pyramids there.

c.900
The kingdom of the Chancay flourishes on Peru's central coast. Its people develop a distinctive pottery style.

Chimu gold spoon

c.1000
The Chimu culture is on the rise in Peru. Its people are skilled weavers, goldsmiths, and architects. They build their capital at Chan Chan, on the coast. The Chimu are eventually conquered by the Incas.

Moctezuma I in his royal attire

c.1300
The Incas begin to expand their empire throughout the central Andes. They are ruled by Viracocha, the first major Inca empire builder.

c.1325
The Aztecs found the city of Tenochtitlan (present-day Mexico City) on an island in Lake Texcoco.

c.1400–1470
Both the Aztec and Inca empires expand rapidly. In 1426, the Aztecs make an alliance with neighbouring cities to help concentrate power in Aztec emperor Itzcoatl's hands. They establish a vast trading empire, and build spectacular temples and pyramids. By 1500, there are more than 10 million Aztec citizens. The Inca empire is also growing. Around 1438, Viracocha dies; Pachacuti, his successor, expands the Inca empire north to present-day Ecuador. The Incas develop a massive road network covering more than 30,000 km (19,000 miles). Relay runners stationed along the network carry urgent messages and military orders back and forth along the entire route.

1440–1468
Aztec emperor Moctezuma I and his army take control of large areas of eastern Mexico.

c.1450
The Inca city of Machu Picchu is built on a remote mountain ridge above the Urubamba River in Peru.

1455
A huge temple is built to the Aztec war god *Huizilopochtli* in Tenochtitlan.

1470
The collapse of the Chimu culture in northern Peru.

1486–1502
The rule of the Aztec emperor Ahuitzotl. The Aztec empire is at the height of its power in Mexico under Ahuitzotl's reign.

1513
Spanish explorer Vasco de Balboa crosses the Central American mainland and becomes the first European to see the Pacific Ocean.

Guaman Poma used drawings in his book, such as this one of a patient visiting a healer, because he felt that pictures were as persuasive as words

Cortés

1519
Spanish explorer and soldier Hernándo Cortés and a band of 500 men reach the Aztec capital of Tenochtitlan. The Aztec emperor Moctezuma II greets him as an honoured guest, but Cortés betrays him, arresting him and killing hundreds of Aztec nobles. The remaining Aztecs revolt the following year, but Cortés eventually prevails and the Aztec empire falls.

1532–1533
With fewer than 200 armed soldiers fighting alongside him, the Spanish warrior Francisco Pizarro attacks the Inca emperor Atahualpa as he marches with his entourage to his coronation. Everyone is killed apart from Atahualpa; his life is spared on the condition that he pay a ransom in silver and gold. Atahualpa hands over the treasure and is promptly strangled.

1542
The Spanish establish a capital at Merida, and the Mayan resistance comes to an end.

1615
Felipe Guaman Poma de Ayala, a native Inca, completes his 1,200-page work, *The First New Chronicle and Good Government*, illustrated with 400 pen-and-ink drawings of Inca and colonial life. He addresses the work to King Philip III of Spain, hoping to seek reform of Spanish colonial governance in order to save the Andean peoples from the destructive forces of colonialism.

Page from Guaman Poma's book

Find out more

THE CULTURES OF THE Aztecs, Incas, and Maya may have disappeared, but the wealth of relics and ruins left behind reveal much about these ancient peoples and their times. If you are able to visit Central or South America, you can explore the sites of these once-thriving cities and follow in the footsteps of the people who lived there. But there are plenty of other ways to learn more about these cultures. The Internet offers virtual tours of places such as ancient temples and sacred cities. Many museums contain excellent collections from these areas.

ENJOY A TREAT TO EAT
If you are hungry to learn more about the cultures you have read about in this book, try a taste of traditional Central and South American cuisine. Many restaurants feature foods based on the same staples – maize, squash, and beans – that fed the Aztecs, Incas, and Maya. Try your hand at cooking a traditional dish, such as tacos.

THE INCA TRAIL
Many of the sites sacred to the ancient Americans are now popular tourist destinations. For example, you can trek along the Inca Trail in Peru to the sacred Inca city of Machu Picchu. The Spanish invaders at the time of the conquest and during centuries of colonial rule had no idea that the city was even there. Machu Picchu is now a World Heritage site and has thousands of visitors each day.

SOUNDS OF THE PAST
Music was an important part of ancient South American and Mesoamerican religious rituals. Today, folk musicians keep the sounds of the past alive, performing traditional music on modern replicas of instruments used by Aztec, Inca, and Mayan musicians. These musicians perform in traditional costume. Check the Internet to find out if a group will be performing at a cultural festival near you.

USEFUL WEBSITES

www.mesoweb.com
Explore the cultures of Mesoamerica

www.ancientmexico.com
The history of ancient Mexico, with an interactive map

www.ancientperu.com
An in-depth look at the Inca universe

www.pbs.org/conquistadors
The story of Spain's crusading adventurers

www.ballgame.org
The Mesoamerican ball-game brought vividly to life

AZTEC DANCERS
Traditional Aztec dance troupes wear vivid costumes lavished with gold and silver embroidery, and elaborate feather headdresses. These dancers are performing at a Native American heritage festival in the United States. Check listings or the Internet to find out if any traditional dance troupes are making an international tour.

Places to Visit

THE BRITISH MUSEUM, LONDON, UK
The museum's gallery devoted to pre-Hispanic cultures in Mesoamerica includes Mixtec codices, sculptures, and a famous collection of Mixtec–Aztec turquoise mosaics.

WORLD MUSEUM, LIVERPOOL, UK
In this museum's World Cultures Gallery, visitors can see pages from the Codex Fejérváry-Mayer, one of the few surviving codices that date from before the destruction of Tenochtitlan. The gallery also includes jewellery, sculptures, and artefacts from the Mayan civilization.

MUSEUM OF ARCHAEOLOGY AND ANTHROPOLOGY, CAMBRIDGE, UK
This museum includes objects from the Moche, Nazca, and Chimu cultures.

MUSEO NACIONAL DE ANTROPOLOGÍA, MEXICO CITY, MEXICO
This museum contains possibly the world's greatest collection of objects related to the Maya. Its interactive kiosks tell the stories behind some 500 important objects on display.

METROPOLITAN MUSEUM OF ART, NEW YORK, USA
The museum's collection from the ancient Americas spans a 3,500 year period. It includes the world's most comprehensive collection of American gold.

VISIT A MUSEUM
Many art and anthropology museums feature important works from the Aztec, Inca, and Mayan civilizations. A museum collection might include examples of textiles, pottery, metalwork, featherwork, basketry, and artefacts crafted from precious stones. Check with travel books or use the Internet to find the best permanent collections (some of which are listed in the box, top right). Also look out for travelling exhibitions from museums in Central and South America.

TRAVEL TO ANCIENT SITES
Exploring the lands of the Aztecs, Incas, or Maya can be an awe-inspiring experience. These tourists are climbing a pyramid in Mexico. Use the Internet to find sites open to visitors. Joining a group tour may give you access to more sites, as well as a valuable commentary from tour guides.

Glossary

ADOBE A traditional building material made from clay, straw, and water, formed into blocks and dried.

AGAVE A tropical American plant with tough, sword-shaped leaves and flowers in tall spikes. In Mesoamerica, the plant's fibres were woven into cloth; people also sucked the sap directly from the plant.

Agave plant

ALPACA A member of the llama family from the South American Andes Mountains. Alpaca hair fibre is prized for the soft, lightweight, yet extremely warm wool that can be woven from it.

ARMADILLO A burrowing, nocturnal mammal covered in strong, horny plates; eaten by Mesoamerican peoples.

ATOLE A mush or thin porridge made with maize, popular in Mesoamerica. The Incas ate a similar dish, called *capia*.

CACAO A tropical evergreen tree. Its dried and partially fermented beans are removed from their pods and processed to make chocolate, cocoa powder, and cocoa butter.

CALPULLI An Aztec neighbourhood with shared rights and responsibilities among the households. The *calpulli* was the basic unit of Aztec society.

CHACMOOL A Mesoamerican sculpture of a reclining figure holding a bowl on its lap or stomach. The bowl is thought to be a receptacle for holding blood and human hearts after a sacrifice.

CHASQUIS In Moche society, a runner who carried messages from one place to another.

CHINAMPAS In Aztec agriculture, narrow strips of land built in swampy lakes, with canals running between them. Each *chinampa* was built with layers of plants cut from the lake and fertile soil from the lake bed.

CODEX An ancient type of book, made of bark paper from the fig tree, cloth, or animal skin folded like a concertina; the name comes from *caudex*, the Latin for "tree bark".

COMAL A large clay disc used for cooking *tortillas* over an open fire.

CONQUEST The acquisition of a territory and its people by force.

CONQUISTADOR One of the 16th-century Spanish explorers who conquered lands in the Americas.

COPAL A brittle, aromatic resin burned as an incense offering in ancient times; now used in varnishes.

DOUBLOON An old Spanish gold coin.

EMBROIDERY The act of embellishing a fabric or garment with a decorative pattern using hand-stitched needlework.

ENCOMENDERO A privileged Spanish colonist during the Spanish conquest of the Americas. The *encomenderos* became an early colonial aristocracy.

FRESCO From the Italian word for "fresh," the technique of painting on wet plaster so that the pigments are absorbed by the plaster, becoming part of the wall itself. A form of fresco that was employed by the artisans of Teotihuacan.

FUNERARY MASK A mask, typically made of metal, that was sometimes placed on the faces of Inca mummies before burial.

Mesoamerican glyph carved in stone

GLYPH A picture used to represent a word or a group of words.

GOURD Any of a group of inedible, vine-growing fruits with hard rinds.

GREENSTONE A dark green, metamorphic rock that owes its colouring to the presence of the mineral chlorite.

HIEROGLYPHIC WRITING A system of writing in which the characters consist of realistic or stylized pictures of actual objects, animals, or humans, rather than letters or words.

HUACAS In the Andean regions, a variety of shrines and objects and the natural forces associated with them.

Detail from Codex Cospi, an Aztec calendar, showing a god attacking an ocelot warrior

JAGUAR A large, spotted cat of tropical America, similar to the leopard.

KERO A drinking vessel, made of metal or wood, traditionally used in Andean feasts.

LABRET A plug inserted through a piercing below the bottom lip.

Jade labret from Mesoamerica

LOOM A machine used to weave yarn into a fabric.

MACUAHUITL One of the Aztecs' main weapons; a wooden club edged with sharp obsidian blades.

MAGUEY A type of agave plant.

MAIZE A tall, annual, cereal grass bearing kernels on large ears of corn; a staple food in Mexico, and Central and South America.

MESOAMERICA The region of Mexico and Central America historically inhabited by the Aztecs, Maya, and related cultures.

METLATL A grinding stone, usually made from volcanic stone such as basalt. *Metlatl* were commonly found in the Mesoamerican kitchen, and are still used today.

MUMMY A body embalmed and dried and wrapped for burial.

MUMMY BUNDLE A Mesoamerican mummy wrapped in textiles or reed matting and tied with ropes.

OBSIDIAN A volcanic glass that may be clear, black, brown, or green. Obsidian is a prized material for making tools, because it can be chipped into a sharp point.

OCELOT A natural wildcat of Central and South America with a dark-spotted, brown coat.

Incan mummy bundle

ONYX A semiprecious stone that is black and white and made up of layers.

PATOLLI An Aztec board game that is very similar to modern-day backgammon.

PECCARY A nocturnal, pig-like wild animal of North and South America.

PONCHO A blanket-like cloak, with a slit in the middle for the head.

PYRAMID A massive memorial with a square base and four triangular sides.

QUETZAL A large tropical bird of Central and South America with golden-green and scarlet feathers.

QUETZALCOATL A legendary plumed or feathered serpent, worshipped by the Maya as a god of nature.

QUINOA A tiny, round, ivory-coloured whole grain used by the Incas, and still eaten today. It is a complete source of dietary protein.

QUIPU An Inca counting device consisting of a length of cord held horizontally, with various knotted strings hanging down. Information was recorded according to the number of knots tied in the strings.

RITUAL The name for any customary observance or practice common to a people.

SACRIFICE The act of killing an animal or person in order to please a deity.

SARCOPHAGUS A stone coffin, or a stone container housing a coffin and a mummy.

Tzompantli at Chichen Itza

SPINDLE A stick or pin used to twist the yarn in spinning wool.

TEMPLE A religious structure built for the worship of a deity.

TERRACING In agriculture, a series of levels on a hillside, one above the other, used to greatly reduce the water erosion of soil.

TERRACOTTA An unglazed fired clay, used for architectural features, ornaments, vessels, and to create sculptures.

TURQUOISE An opaque, blue, semiprecious stone with a porous, soft texture, prized in Mesoamerica.

TZOMPANTLI A skull rack placed outside a temple; for example, to hold the skulls of sacrificial victims.

UICTLI An essential farmer's tool; a digging stick made from strong, longlasting wood with a long, broad blade carved into one end.

ULAMA The sacred ball-game, played in Mesoamerica by the Aztecs, Maya, and earlier civilizations.

VICUÑA A small, wild, cud-chewing animal similar to a llama but smaller; valued for its fleecy coat.

VIGESIMAL Relating to, or based on, the number 20, as in Mayan mathematics.

WHORL A circular arrangement of three or more leaves or flowers, equally spaced around the stem like spokes on a wheel.

The long, flowing tail feathers were prized for use in religious ceremonies

Quetzal

Index

Acknowledgements

The publisher would like to thank:
Dra. Mari Carmen Serra Puche and all those who helped with photography at Museo Nacional de Antropologia, Mexico City; Professor Eduardo Matos Moctezuma and all those who helped with photography at the Great Temple Museum, Mexico City (INAH.-CNCA.-Mex); Phil Watson at the Birmingham Museum; Maureen Barry at the Royal Museum of Scotland; British Museum; Pitt Rivers Museum; Cambridge University Museum of Archaeology and Anthropology; Reynaldo Izquierdo (Mexico) and Eugene Staken for photographic assistance; Sue Giles at the City of Bristol Museum; Jabu Mahlangu, Manisha Patel, Jill Plank, and Sharon Spencer for design assistance; Katharine Thompson; Lic. Victor Hugo Vidal Alvarez and Lic. Javier García Martinez at the Tourist Office, Mexico City; John Woodcock and Andrew Nash for illustrations; Carol Davis for art-editing on the jacket.
Additional photography: Geoff Dann (24ar); Steve Gorton (39al); Peter Hayman (60cl; 60c); Dave King (61bc); James Stephenson (14bl; 62-63 top; 63bl); Jerry Young (61ar; 61cl).
Index Lynn Bresler
Proofreading Miranda Smith
Wallchart Peter Radcliffe, Steve Setford

The publisher would like to thank the following for their kind permission to reproduce their photographs:

(Key: a-above; b-below/bottom; c-centre; f-far; l-left; r-right; t-top)

Ancient Art and Architecture Collection: 51 acr; The Art Archive: 38 ar; Biblioteca Medicea Laurenziana, Florence: 14acl, 48al, 51c; Biblioteca Nazionale Centrale, Florence 21al/Photo Scala: 35cl, 37al; Bibliothèque de l'Assemblée nationale, Paris: 30bl, 56bl; Bridgeman Art Library: Biblioteca Nacional, Madrid: 62cl; British Library: 17c, 19al; British Museum: 54bl; e.t. archive 26c, (detail, Diego Rivera 'Tarascan Civilisation') 42cr; Museum of Mankind (detail: Diego Rivera 'Cultivation of Maize') 24bc, (detail: Diego Rivera 'La Civilisation Zapotheque') 9bl, (detail, Diego Rivera 'The market of Tenochtitlan') 53bl; Private Collection: 63br; Bristol Museums and Art Gallery: 29br, 46c, 49bl, 62br; © The Trustees of the British Museum: 33 acr, 47 ar; J. L. Charmet: 37bl, 44bl; Bruce Coleman Ltd: 16ar, 19ar, 60ar, 61al, 61ac; Corbis: Archivo Iconografico, S.A. 67tr; Nathan Benn 66tr; Bettmann 67bl; 67br; Jonathan Blair 69br; Bohemian Nomad Picturemakers 64tl; Don Conrad 64bl; Sergio Dorantes 70-71; Macduff Everton 68–69; Randy Faris 66b; Kevin Fleming 69tl; Werner Forman 64–65, 70b; Angelo Hornak 65tr; Charles & Josette Lenars 67tl; Gianni Dagli Orti 64br, 65cl, 69cl; Jose Luis Pelaez, Inc. 68tl; Bill Ross 71br; Kevin Schafer 65bc; Roman Soumar 68bl; e.t. archive: 22c, 32al, 38c, 40cr, 51br, 57c, 58al; Archaeological Museum, Lima: 20bl, 38br, 51br, 55br; Arteaga Collection, Lima: 15cr; Museo Ciudad Mexico/Sapieha: 12ac; University Museum, Cuzco: 10ar; Mary Evans Picture Library: 33cl, 45ac, 62bl/Explorer: 40al; Werner Forman Archive/Anthropology Museum, Veracruz: 9ar; Getty Images: AFP: 69bl Robert Harding Picture Library: 11bl, 17ac, 18cr, 18bl; Michael Holford: 16c, 17ar, 33bl, 54br, 56al; Hutchison Library: 59ar; Dorig: 7ar, 30cl, 34a; Pate: 17acr; Linda Whitwam © CONACULTA-INAH-MEX. Authorized reproduction by the Instituto Nacional de Antropologia e Historia: 70tr Edward H. Merrin Gallery, New York: 45ar; Museum Für Vülkerkunde, Vienna: 49cr; National Geographic Stock: Marial Stenzel: 35 ar; National Museum of Anthropology, Mexico City: 53al; Peter Newark: 59acr; NHPA: Bernard: 13acl; Woodfall: 19b; Rietberg Museum, Zurich: 10bl; Nick Saunders/Barbara Heller: 18c, 19acl, 23al, 31ar, 63ar; Photo Scala: Museo d'America, Madrid: 6br; South American Pictures: 13al, 13br, 15bc, 18cl, 18ar; 27al, 27acl, 30ar, 33ar, 34c, 40bc, 42al, 43ac, 57ar; Hubert Stadler: 68cr; Michel Zabé: 30–31, 36bl, 47acl, 49c, 50al, 51ar, 52bl, 52c/NMA, Mexico City: 29al.

Wallchart:
Dorling Kindersley: Dave Rudkin © Dorling Kindersley, Courtesy of the Birmingham Museum and Art Galleries 1bc, 1crb (bag), 1fcra; © The British Museum 1br (coins); Michel Zabe © CONACULTA-INAH-MEX. Authorized reproduction by the Instituto Nacional de Antropologia e Historia. 1bl, 1ca, 1clb, 1crb (book), 1tl; Andy Crawford © Dorling Kindersley, Courtesy of the Pitt Rivers Museum, University of Oxford 1cb; © Dorling Kindersley, Courtesy of the University Museum of Archaeology and Anthropology, Cambridge 1crb, 1crb (counting device); Demetrio Carrasco © Rough Guides/Dorling Kindersley 1cl; Michel Zabe 1cr; Getty Images: Bridgeman Art Library 1br; Robert Harding 1tr

Jacket:
Front: Dorling Kindersley: CONACULTA-INAH-MEX. Authorized reproduction by the Instituto Nàcional de Antropologia e Historia tc. **Michael Holford:** b. **Back: Dorling Kindersley:** Birmingham Museum and Art Galleries crb; CONACULTA-INAH-MEX. Authorized reproduction by the Instituto Nacional de Antropologia e Historia cra, l, fcra, bl; Royal Museum of Scotland, Edinburgh tc; Michel Zabe crb (necklace).

All other images © Dorling Kindersley.
For further information see:
www.dkimages.com